Titanic Submarine

The Unsolved Mystery of the Titanic Submersible

(Oceangate Latest Findings There is to Know About the Tragedy Story, Mission Crews and Lots More)

Jared Watson

Published By **Andrew Zen**

Jared Watson

All Rights Reserved

Titanic Submarine: The Unsolved Mystery of the Titanic Submersible (Oceangate Latest Findings There is to Know About the Tragedy Story, Mission Crews and Lots More)

ISBN 978-1-7752884-1-1

No part of this guidebook shall be reproduced in any form without permission in writing from the publisher except in the case of brief quotations embodied in critical articles or reviews.

Legal & Disclaimer

The information contained in this book is not designed to replace or take the place of any form of medicine or professional medical advice. The information in this book has been provided for educational & entertainment purposes only.

The information contained in this book has been compiled from sources deemed reliable, and it is accurate to the best of the Author's knowledge; however, the Author cannot guarantee its accuracy and validity and cannot be held liable for any errors or omissions. Changes are periodically made to this book. You must consult your doctor or get professional medical advice before using any of the suggested remedies, techniques, or information in this book.

Upon using the information contained in this book, you agree to hold harmless the Author from and against any damages, costs, and expenses, including any legal fees potentially resulting from the application of any of the information provided by this guide. This disclaimer applies to any damages or injury caused by the use and application, whether directly or indirectly, of any advice or information presented, whether for breach of contract, tort, negligence, personal injury, criminal intent, or under any other cause of action.

You agree to accept all risks of using the information presented inside this book. You need to consult a professional medical practitioner in order to ensure you are both able and healthy enough to participate in this program.

Table Of Contents

Chapter 1: Setting Sail 1

Chapter 2: The Fateful Encounter 16

Chapter 3: The Rescue Efforts 31

Chapter 4: Legacy And Remembrance ... 42

Chapter 5: Tragic Story Of Devastation Following 59

Chapter 6: Titanic Short History 81

Chapter 7: Titanic Submarine 101

Chapter 8: Hamish Harding 113

Chapter 9: Stockton Rush The Ceo And Co-Founder Of Ocean 127

Chapter 10: The Titanic And Its Wreck . 139

Chapter 11: The Missing Submarine 154

Chapter 12: The Theories 162

Chapter 13: The Impact 173

Chapter 13: The Future 180

Chapter 1: Setting Sail

The Dream of the Unsinkable

Friends, let me to bring you back to the glorious and awe-inspiring era of titanic's majestic beginning. Take a deep breath and imagine the Titanic as a vessel that's incredible and majestic that it's been declared to be invincible! It was not a normal vessel; it represented the fulfillment of a vision and representation of human creativity as well as the constant pursuit to achieve the highest level of excellence.

Are you even able to imagine the sheer determination and unflinching faith required for such an amazing feat? The Titanic's designers dared to test the limits of conventional knowledge. They mastered how to build ships, as well as combining knowledge and creativity to build a ship which could effortlessly navigate through the ocean's vast expanse.

The globe was filled with anticipation and excitement when news about this incredible invention spread rapidly. The first voyage of the incredible ship that would forever inscribe the Titanic's name Titanic into the saga of time, was looked forward to by an astonished world.

It wasn't only the beauty of nature that caught the collective imagination. The ship also symbolized the beginning of a new century and the triumph of mankind over the odds. The concept of a sinking vessel symbolized our unwavering search for advancement as well as our determination to rise over the limits set upon us. I assure you that nobody can be unlimited at the moment when modern technology was an effortless thing which nobody thought of yet people still had the thought of building a huge vessel.

The Titanic was much more than the name of a vessel. It was also a symbol for potential and hope. It encouraged us to put aside any doubts and look forward to the endless possibilities that lay before the passengers as it served as an extraordinary instance of human capacity.

Think about the amazing lavishness that welcomed all those lucky enough to be able to step onto through the decks of this gorgeous floating castle! First-class accommodation was an absolute example of luxurious that included massive suites, lavish dining rooms and just about every luxury that humans could dream of. It was a realm only for the wealthy, in which the crème de la cream luxuriated in the midst of luxury while they travelled across the huge area in the Atlantic.

Let us not lose sight of the fantasies of people who were looking for an opportunity to start afresh in a new country. In the class of steerage, passengers shared their hopes and dreams of an improved future on the decks below. The ship was full of an array of fantasies due to their enthusiasm and their fire that burned radiantly in spite of their shabby living quarters, and far from luxury living conditions.

My dear friends Let's celebrate the vision of the insinkable which captivated all those who stepped foot on the Titanic when we embarked to embark on this thrilling journey. Let's be proud of the bravery and courage that defied from the shackles of the past and propelled mankind forward. Be prepared for the future that is to come, which will test human resilience and endurance to the examination. If we feel for the heroes of our time, 1517 is lost to the point when the most powerful Titanic vessel Sank.

Take me on a journey through time to witness an old legend come alive and uncover the shocking story behind the tragic sinking of the mighty Titanic ship. The journey will take us through the darkness of the past together, resolving the mystery of fate, and providing insight into the morals that lie behind the most horrific of human tales. Prior to my talk, as to show respect to the Titanic, please bow your head after the shocking announcement of the deaths of five billionaires in the Titanic submersible, confirmed dead as stated by BBC news service on the 23rd of the 23rd of June in 2023. " My Almighty God rest their souls in eternal peace" Amen!

A Voyage of Opulence

Take a cruise on the stunning Titanic and enter into a world filled with extravagant luxury, where excess is the rule. Prepare to travel back into a world where the world was awash with luxury and the rich few could enjoy an orchestra of extravagant and magnificence.

The splendor of the ship drew all attention when it began its voyage. My friends, the top-of-the-line rooms were truly palaces that were floating on water. Imagine walking through the halls which are finished and boasting exquisite wooden work. It's like you're set to go off on a grand adventure only accessible to the most elite because the air has a the sophisticated ambiance.

In the luxurious suites, get ready to be mesmerized by the world of refined luxurious. Silken curtains that stretch from floor to ceiling cover windows with breathtaking perspectives of the ocean to the west. The soft furnishings invite you to relax in their cosy embrace with intricate detailing and slick details add luxury to each and every room. It's a place that combines luxury and comfort, in which every desire remains empty.

Oh my, the lavishness didn't stop there. Imagine walking into lavish dining halls, where innovative culinary awe meets extravagant indulgence. Chefs of the best worked tirelessly in order to create culinary masterpieces that would delight the palates of the very few. The warm and glistening light of crystal chandeliers lit up the table, lighting it with a dazzling glow. decorated with exquisite silverware and sparkling china. Each meal was an absolute work of art, a concert of tastes that delighted the senses and danced the tongue.

When the Titanic The Titanic, the social scene also became opulent. The first-class lounges were where celebrities gathered in vibrant gatherings with an atmosphere of elegant elegance. Imagine sitting on luxurious velvet sofas, while you listen to the sweet sound of the grand piano. The laughter and lively conversation suffused the air when guests enjoyed being with their friends and enjoyed the thrill of the present.

We shouldn't forget the hopes of the people who lived on the lower decks even as extravagant was the order of the day for those lucky. Even though the "steerage class" didn't have the same opulence as those who were who were above them, their spirit weren't less flamboyant. Rooms in the common areas were ablaze of activity, with a variety of hopes and cultures that woven together into the tangle of hope. In spite of the restrictions which society was trying to enforce and impose, humanity's spirit of tenacity was shining brightly.

Friends, let's get absorbed in the true story of splendor that was played out at these sacred sites when we traverse the decks of Titanic. Take a moment and be amazed by the splendor of the ship, its extravagantness, and the sheer majesty of a time in which the limits of luxury were defied. Let's not forget, however, that this vessel held the dreams and hopes of many people buried beneath the facade of splendor.

The world of Titanic stood tall in a testament to the desire for luxury and awe-inspiring beauty that was once present. Take me along as we journey through the grand halls and discover the mystery of that place. As a group, we'll look at the vast tapestry of splendor and explore the profound impact this trip affected every person who traveled on her stunning decks.

People are from All Walks of Life

There is a wonderful mix of souls from around the globe as we read the voyage of the Titanic. Many people from all different walks of life embarked to sea seeking the thrill of a lifetime, peace or new beginnings starting from the busy city of London to the pristine coastlines of Ireland.

Within the splendor of first society, prestigious figures from the upper class enjoyed the lavish surroundings. The vast lounges were where the top businessmen, politicians and famous people gathered to socialize into the luxurious ambience. They enjoyed extravagant luxury and pleasures provided to them as the vessel travelled through in the North Atlantic.

When this happened an eclectic group of passengers from the class of steerage embarked on a voyage to having a brighter future at the lower levels. People and women who had dreams of progress and an eagerness for new perspectives come from various countries. They shared common places that were filled in excitement and friendship while they shared stories or jokes.

They also shared their shared bond of optimism.

While the Titanic was sailing across the Atlantic The ship's position was the most important factor in the passenger's ever-changing journey. The ship left Southampton, England, and was able to arrive at Cherbourg, France, for the first stop. It was here that many more passengers boarded. It then headed towards Queenstown (now Cobh), Ireland and brought in more passengers before sailing for its disastrous crossing of the Atlantic Ocean towards New York City, the vessel's ultimate destination.

The interaction of passengers from various kinds of backgrounds and social classes made a vibrant microcosmic of the society aboard the Titanic. People from different backgrounds became friends, and formed bonds which crossed social lines. The luxurious ship was a catalyst for equality that brought people closer within shared space and establishing connections that would forever tie their destiny.

It was not known they would be on board the Titanic was a time of risk and tragedy. The highly praised engineering marvel floated across the freezing oceans of North Atlantic, its passengers ignorant of the impending catastrophe that lurked in the dark. The setting was awaited for a dramatic battle between humanity's endurance and the relentless elements of the natural world.

Class Distinctions

The life aboard the Titanic unfolded like the story of two worlds, as it cruised across the ocean. The journey showed the complicated network of class differences which made the distinction between classes evident.

The passengers of the first class luxuriated in an unrestricted paradise in the upper decks the vessel. They dressed in most elegant attire and walked with an elegant grace with their elegance and elegance to be easily perceived. The places they played were lounges and salons which were a place where conversations flowed effortlessly alongside the abundance of bubbly and laughter, accompanied by the crackling of crystal glasses.

First-class guests savored the ultimate luxuriousness in the extravagant suites. Silk drapes bobbed gently with the breeze of the ocean, giving panorama views of the infinite horizon. They were enveloped by a world of stunning splendor as the intricate design and lavish decor attracted people to give in to their enticing hug.

However, beyond the splendor of the class that was first, there was a completely different experience waiting for. On the lower decks, passengers of the steerage class found themselves within a totally different realm. Though their rooms were less modest and the hallways more narrow, their hearts were filled with the spirit of determination.

In the common areas of the lower decks is a colorful tapestry of different cultures and unfulfilled dreams.. Family members gathered, sharing laughter and jokes, while strengthening connections in preparation for the upcoming storm. While the scents of a variety of food items filled the air, the dining areas were buzzing filled with energy. The air was filled with hope and each person held the belief that this journey will lead them towards a better future, regardless of the obstacles they had to face.

When you boarded the Titanic it was clear that there was a gap in class that was evident not only in the physical locations, but also the relationships between people. People of the upper class had a privileged social circle which often talked about important connections and achievements in their conversation. They believed in the myth of being invincible, believing their social standing protected them from any dangers to come.

However, the barriers between classes weren't insurmountable. Random encounters and moments of shared time have blurred lines of difference providing glimpses into humanity's connectivity. Talks between a steerage-class person who was a dreamer as well as a first-class nobleman revealed shared dreams goals, worries, and dreams that transcended the limits of social status. The essence of human experience was reflected in the tiniest of connections, acting as a reminder of how all of us are on our common journey in the world.

The passengers on the Titanic, although separated by class, but joined to pursue an unforgettable adventure, were completely unaware of their imminent disasters when they went on to cruise. The threads that held the lives of their passengers were hid from view by the sparkling passageways and busy hallways. those threads would later be tested and ripped apart when fate dealt the cruel blow.

Chapter 2: The Fateful Encounter

A Night to Remember

The Titanic cruised across the frigid seas as the cold night breeze whispered the secrets of the vast and deep North Atlantic. It was an unforgettable night like the rest, one that was remembered as the epitomize of human achievement and heartbreaking loss which would be remembered as a tragic event which would eventually be written into the long history of mankind.

The large ship briskly cruised throughout the dark night on April 14th 1912. They had no idea of the imminent disaster that lay ahead beneath the serene waters while they soaked up the breathtaking beauty and richness surrounding them. The Titanic is a testimony to humanity's insane ambition, carried souls from every walk of life. Each with their own goals and hopes.

The crew kept an attentive watching the clock as it approached midnight, ensuring the ship's safe passage through the freezing waters.

Officers and captains gazed through the night looking out to look for signs of risk. Icebergs swam across the halls, causing the feeling of anticipation that hung throughout the room.

In a bizarre twist of fate, the warning went out. A faint glimpse of an iceberg appeared in the direction of the ship. The voices of the people in charge of steering the ship towards safe were punctuated by panic when they tried to steer the massive ship away from danger. Engines roared and churned the sea below in a rush of adrenaline.

However, it was already way too far too late.

The Titanic with her magnificent body slicing through waves, collided with an frozen iceberg. It was an invisibly force that shattered the illusion imperviousness. The Titanic's entire structure twitched as if it was woken off of its sleeping state by an external force. Invisible gashes ripped across the hull, opening up icy waters to penetrate the once-inaccessible fortress.

The cabin's inhabitants, awoken by the unsettling tremors were able to leave their cabins, and looked shocked. Incredulity and fear mingled as they stood on the deck. They were awestruck by a scene which was unimaginable. The huge, icy beast that brutally destroyed the vessel loomed over them, providing an inspiring reminder of just the fragile human effort that can be.

The reality of the tragedy flooded into our hearts, chaos broke out. The children and the women who's faces were stained by a mix of fear and despair, were swiftly taken to lifeboats. The majority of those in lifeboats of escape were able to make it through the darkness that was unforgiving that left behind a vast sea of souls battling imminent doom.

Within the midst of the chaos, strength and selfless actions were shown. Even in the face of danger courageous people -- crew members as well as passengers--led other people to safety and gave comfort even in the face of unbearable horror. They faced a sea of despair, showing the resilience of human spirit, even in facing of imminent disaster.

Once proud and invincible Titanic began sinking into the cold depths of the Atlantic as minutes transformed into hours. The beauty that had attracted all the world seemed to be an unsettling silhouette in the stars of the sky. The vessel, which previously been an icon of human progress and achievement, was now an example of the fragility the human condition is.

So, as evening wore on as the night grew darker, the Titanic disappeared into the sea, carrying passengers' desires and hopes of the passengers that were on board. In the end, however, the North Atlantic took its cruel reward, leaving nothing except stories of sustenance as well as the weight of unimaginable loss.

An evening to be remembered, dear ones, a night that served as an introspective reminder of humanity's spirit that is unstoppable and the consequences of arrogance against nature's power. The evening of April 14th, 1912 would be recorded as being one memorable night of the year. Once again, may the souls that were lost in the tragedy remain in peace forever. Amen!

Warnings Ignored.

The vast North Atlantic stretched out before the Titanic when it embarked on its initial voyage. the gloomy stage in which fate and destiny were bound to meet. However, in the midst of the splendor and excitement that hung in the atmosphere, there were also subtle alerts, signals which were ignored by dear friends, securing the fate of this massive vessel.

The days prior to the trip in the days leading up to the voyage, reports had surfaced of icebergs floating along the route of the vessel. The most experienced mariners and sailors advised that prudence should be the rule in the face of these dangerous obstacles. But, the cautions were met with a lack of concern as if there was no reason to believe that the vessel was invincible. ship.

The people responsible for ensuring Titanic's safety during its voyage received numerous alerts about ice via an electronic telegraph while the vessel was sailing. The messages announced the existence of ice fields as well as specific icebergs in the vicinity. However, these warnings were ignored in the search for fame, and eventually drowned in a sea distracting and uninvolved.

An illusion of security resulted in the crew losing their focus from the tragedy that took place on the 14th of April 1912. The wireless network operators tirelessly broadcast messages to passengers in social interaction but perhaps not knowing the fate of a lot of people.

In the absence of any passengers' awareness that night, the Titanic ran into the darkness towards the danger of a dangerous confrontation. The iceberg appeared over the edge of the horizon, and threatened to cause disaster due to its terrifying appearance. The ship continued to follow the course, however, supported by the feeling of unshakeable security and invincibility.

Night engulfed the ship and encased it in darkness that was inky. A watchman sat on top of the crow's trough, straining to gaze out at the distant and look for signs of danger. The absence of night light and the calm of the ocean combined to prevent the approaching iceberg not being observed until it was far too far too late.

The shivering sound echoed through the steel frame of the ship as a stark warning of what could be the result if cautions are not taken into consideration. The first shockwaves changed the fate of the vessel into one that was awe-inspiring into an unavoidable tragedy. The Titanic had sustained devastating injuries due to the iceberg that left its fragile underbelly vulnerable to the ocean's relentless attack.

It is possible that the outcome would be different had the cautionary principle prevailed over arrogance and if the warnings were followed. But, the Titanic as well as its crew suffered the fate of a combination of circumstance and hubris and forced them to engage in the midst of a gruelling battle with the elements.

As we contemplate this chapter of Titanic's tale, we hope that it will serve as a tragic warning of the risks of negligence and the devastating consequence of ignoring warnings within our heads. As a result of the tragic incident we will have to grapple with possibilities of what might be, and also the lasting lesson of arrogance that could be the catalyst to tragedies.

The Tragic Impact

When the Titanic injured by the cruel grasp of the iceberg and struggled to escape her imminent fate and the dark night was suffused with fear and fear. The collision had triggered the chain of tragic events which would alter the course of human time and forever leave a lasting impression on the souls and thoughts of those who were witness to the disaster.

When the cold waters inundated all the cabins on the ship in panic, the heart of both crew and passengers. As the full scope of the disaster began to emerge the shocking reality of what a dire state their condition was. The streets once bustling with joy and merriment, their passageways were filled with despair and despair.

Lifeboats, the vessels of hope and redemption have become a vital lifeline to avoid imminent disaster. But they were overpowered by the job at hand. The Titanic is a giant made of steel and hope was designed to house much more lifeboats than actually aboard. When the pressure increased, the grim reality began to dawn: there was not enough lifeboats available for every person.

The most amazing acts of kindness popped up in the midst of heartbreaking and chaotic situations, shining like light during the dark. They put the safety of those around them prior to their own. They struggled with elements in order to reach safety while sailing through the treacherous waters, grasping their hands with a firm grip on the rowing oars.

Travelers too showed remarkable courage and grit. Faced with the imminent danger, they assisted fellow travelers, giving messages of comfort as well as acts of kindness that transcended boundaries of status and class. As fathers battled the rising storm and tried to shield their family members from brutal cold, mothers soothed their kids, reassuring that help was on the way.

For every tale of heroic acts There were countless stories of despair and loss. Families split up by the cruel hand of destiny. The friends hung on to each other and their hope was fading each passing second. The cold seas relentlessly took lives, taking out the dreams and hopes of those who embarked on this terrifying trip.

When the bow of the ship sank into the depths of the ocean and the symphonic sounds of music echoed through the space. The group continued to perform even though they realized how futile they were to go on. They reverberated throughout the ship, sending the message of unification and courage to withstand the threat of catastrophe.

The Titanic finally gave in to the ferocious grip of the sea's depths as a final gesture of surrender. The hopes and desires of those who had been with her, the huge vessel, once a emblem of ambition for mankind and an engineering marvel, sank under the ocean's waves. In the North Atlantic, now a huge and solemn cemetery, held the remains of an earlier era.

The Titanic's sinking was broadcast across the globe like a mournful music of despair and grief. Newspapers raced to present readers with to know the details of the tragedy that occurred, intensifying the shock and sorrow which resonated across communities far and far.

The news was an unwelcome shock for travelers in the United States, where a significant portion were originated from. Families eagerly anticipated news from their loved ones doing their best to ensure their lives. In the process of conveying the weight of news coming from the depths of the ocean the telegrams and letters grew into channels of joy and sadness. The people who heard of each news item felt pain as the scale of the loss became apparent.

The impact of the Titanic's sinking extended beyond the human realm as well as the political and economic spheres. The tragedy sparked a worldwide examination of the laws governing marine safety and led to adopting stricter regulations designed to prevent similar catastrophes from happening again. In a shift to making sure that people are safe travelling across oceans, there were improvements introduced to ship designs as well as communication technologies and procedures for emergencies.

In the aftermath of the tragedy following the tragedy, there was an international expression of sorrow and solidarity for the families of victims as well as for the survivors. The community came together to offer assistance and comfort as efforts to help were being planned. the funds were raised, and money was collected. All over the globe mourned for the deaths that took their lives in that tragic night that turned the loss that was the Titanic into a worldwide tragedy which transcended national borders.

The families and their loved ones who were that were lost, the sorrow of loss was followed by the arduous task of reconstructing their lives. The economic challenges resulted from the loss of breadwinners and other providers as families had to contend with fear and uncertainty as well as the daunting prospect of moving forward. Humanity's resilience was evident in the midst of turmoil and grief when survivors and communities discovered the courage to stand in rebuilding and honour the memories of the people who died.

The tragedy of sinking the Titanic provided an eloquent reminder of the fragility of life as well as the fleeting quality of our human pursuits. It brought about vulnerability and provoked reflection on the part of society and individuals. This incident forever changed the way we view risk, safety as well as the value of our lives. It left an indelible impression on our society.

We, dear friends, must pay tribute to those who lost their lives and celebrate the courage of the survivors in the wake of the devastating results from the sinking Titanic. Let the lessons learned drawn from their stories be a constant reminder of that life's fragility, and our enduring strength as human spirit. We must embrace compassion, resilience and the perpetual need for a more secure and more connected community to honor their memory. We hope that the lessons learned from this tragedy will aid us in navigating the waters of our lives in the coming years by utilizing caution, compassion and utmost reverence for the immense power and unpredictability of nature.

After this tragic catastrophe, the world would be forever altered. The lessons learned would be absorbed and safety rules for maritime vessels were redesigned. The people who are able to remember the event and have been witnesses to tales of courage in selfless acts, as well as the power that endures the human spirit will always hold an enduring memory of the Titanic within their minds and hearts.

Chapter 3: The Rescue Efforts

Nearby Ships Respond

In the vast North Atlantic, when word of the tragic loss of the Titanic became known, ships around the area became a beacon of hope. The distress messages sent out by the ship's ill-fated vessel were heard and felt in the hearts of all those around the area, sparking an extraordinary display of kindness and bravery.

As the Titanic issued its distress signal several ships were diverted, and the crews preparing to help those who were struggling to survive the cold, icy ocean's wrath. The Carpathia with the leadership by the captain Arthur Rostron, was the first ship to arrive at the scene. Our dearest companions. The crew of the ship sailed through the stormy night in a manner that was precise and determined and a relentless commitment to help people in need.

The magnitude of the disaster began to be apparent as Carpathia came close. The frigid waters were filled with lifeboats that carried survivors who were brought together to share warmth. Carpathia's crew worked hard to get the survivors aboard as they offered comfort and peace in the midst of chaos.

Other ships like the Californian were also responding to the Titanic's distress signal. But due to unfortunate situations and a lack of communication the efforts of these ships fell just short of what they were aiming for. The Californian was near to the wrecked ship, but did not recognize the urgent nature of the incident which left them with regret for their missed chance to save even more lives.

While the search efforts carried forward, survivors on the Carpathia were confronted by the reality of their recent safe haven. After initial relief and shock an underlying sense of sadness arose when they attempted to cope with the huge loss of the survivors. They became close to each other and built a bond of kinship through the heart of tragedy, which could bind them for eternity because of their common experience of the tragic journey of Titanic.

As the rescue vessels were brought to New York City, they received a mix of emotions. A huge crowd of people greeted survivors at the time they boarded an emotional reminder of the effects that the Titanic's sinking caused to the whole world. Families came together, tears of relief mixing with bittersweet happiness, as others confronted the brutal realisation of a future that was that was forever changed by the loss.

The valiant and heroic rescue efforts were not able to alter the brutality of the incident. People demanded explanations, as all over the world mourned the loss of lives. The investigation began to find the causes of the tragedy and to determine the lessons that could be learned from the tragedy. The sinking of the Titanic had ripples all over the maritime sector and prompted a new commitment to the safety of ships and of marine life.

Dear reader, as we reflect on the rescue operation which took place following the Titanic was lost, don't overlook the courage and compassion that those who responded to the call for help. Pay tribute to those who lost their lives and those who survived. Their experiences should provide a glimpse of the strength and goodwill that are at the root of every human being's soul. Also, may they rest in peace.

In the aftermath of this disaster the new regulations were enacted to ensure that future voyages were made using a more thorough understanding of the hazards that exist under the seafloor. The Titanic's tale is still awe-inspiring and serves as a constant reminding us of the value of teamwork, foresight, and an unflinching commitment to the security and well-being of seafarers everywhere.

Emotional Rescue of Survivors

Alongside the rescue efforts that occurred after the sinking of the Titanic it was also a different kind of rescue operation that was designed to heal survivors with broken hearts and weak spirits. The psychological impact on the victims of this tragic event cannot be overstated and those who escaped the icy North Atlantic waters were besieged by a swarm of love and love.

A flurry of emotions washed over survivors when they arrived aboard the Carpathia. The relief was mixed with the grief and gratitude, as well as guilt for the survivor. As they shared their traumas the survivors clung to each other to seek the comfort and acceptance. These bonds created during the darkest hours of sea turned into a lifeline providing a sense of connection in the midst of overwhelming uncertainty.

The entire crew as well as other passengers on board the Carpathia joined forces to help and console the wounded. A warm blanket was thrown over shoulders shaking with fear and hot beverages were offered to ease nerves that were tense, and affectionate words were spoken to ease the pain that was reverberating through their hearts. The complete power of empathy could be seen as strangers were transformed into trusted friends. This was effective in healing physical and mental injuries.

Once they reached New York City, the heartbreaking rescue missions continued. The relief centers were established for survivors to have the opportunity to have a room with food and drink as well as a secure environment where they could share their tales and receive help from others. People who suffered from unimaginable trauma were able to access experts in medicine and counsellors trained to address the physical and mental needs of those who suffered.

Families waiting for the news of their loved ones' deaths leaned on one another with determination and their hearts filled with joy as well as sorrow. The tragic voyage of the Titanic affected the bonds among the survivors who reached out towards their loved ones for support within the warm embrace of their home.

My dear friends The emotional healing was not just a matter of immediate aftereffects. Healing was an ongoing one for many of the survivors. They had to deal with the traumatic images of that night which forever changed their lives, as they carried the guilt of a survivor. Survivor groups and support groups provided a source of support in the months that followed and provided those with the scars, visible or not, a feel of belonging as well as understanding.

Due to the tragic events of the Titanic, all of society gained more empathy and renewed commitment to help those who had been through the tragedy. The legacy of survivors and self-confidence served as a catalyst for change, sparking discussion about the importance of compassion in times of crisis in trauma healing, as well as mental health.

Aftermath and Consequences

The Titanic's sinking forever altered the course of human history. It also caused a string of events significant enough to change the way people travel by vessels in the coming years. There was a sense of mourning throughout all of the globe within the first few days of the tragedy. The impact of the disaster on communities was profound. death of more than 1500 victims, breaking families and breaking the hearts of whole nations. The scale of the catastrophe called for answers, and an investigation began to determine what caused sinking of the "unsinkable" ship.

The aftermath of Titanic's sinking exposed a series of errors and mistakes which led to the magnitude of the disaster. The tragedy was caused by the inadequate capacity of lifeboats as well as a lack of comprehensive safety plan, as well as the false impression of the invincibility of. After the incident the incident, there was a massive public protest that called for change and accountability within the maritime sector.

The investigation progressed and important reforms were enacted in order to ensure that the same disaster never happens once more. It was in this way that the International Convention for the Safety of Life at Sea (SOLAS) was drafted, laying out strict safety standards for passengers on vessels. In order to protect life at sea, the guidelines covered subjects including lifeboats as well as wireless communication technology and compulsory safety exercise.

The Titanic catastrophe caused significant economic damage in addition. Insurers suffered massive damages, as well as lawsuits initiated by the survivors' families against White Star Line, the company who owned the fateful vessel. The financial consequences were felt all over the maritime industry and led to more attention and stricter regulations on shipbuilders, operators as well as insurers.

Additionally it was the Titanic tragedy also destroyed the notion of invincibility which was prevalent in the age of technological progress. It was a stark reminding of the unpredictable and powerful forces of nature that rekindled a sense of appreciation and humility for the pitfalls that lay ahead for anyone who dares to take on the immense ocean.

The Titanic's impact is still evident today through the lessons learned and advances on safety for mariners. It was the catalyst to change and ingenuity that led to advances in the field of communication technology as well as emergency response and designs for ships. The loss of lives in that night of tragedy was the catalyst to make marine transportation safe and secure.

Beyond the security concerns and regulations beyond security and regulations, the Titanic catastrophe had a long-lasting influence on culture. It was a symbol for humanity's arrogance as well as the fragility of our dreams. The story of the voyageurs and their hopes, aspirations and the tragic losses attract the public's attention. The Titanic is immortalized through movies, books and countless artistic interpretations which ensure that the memories of those who lost their lives remains a constant reminder throughout history.

Chapter 4: Legacy And Remembrance

Investigations and Inquiries

The sinking of Titanic did not just prompt immediate changes, but also spurred an unending search for solutions and justice. The investigation and inquiries were launched after the catastrophe to unravel the intricate chain of events that led to the loss of many lives.

Investigations were conducted by the British as well as the American government, which formed panels of experts and experts to investigate the causes of the catastrophe. Each of the British Board of Trade and the US Senate initiated inquiries to discover the root cause, delegate responsible parties, and to prevent further disasters of this kind in the future.

There were a variety of elements which contributed to Titanic's sinking were identified in the course of examinations. One of the most important flaws highlighted was the absence of lifeboats in the ship, disregard of warnings about icebergs and the absence of an effective crisis response plan. The incidents that occurred during that night of terror was well-recorded in the accounts of the crew, survivors as well as industry experts.

The investigation showed that the ship's conception and operations were hampered by an attitude of overconfidence and complacency. These investigations exposed flaws in the standards of shipbuilding and guidelines along with lapses regarding the education and preparation of crew members. The investigation was crucial in finding out the necessity of extensive adjustments to ensure security of any future trips.

The discoveries and suggestions that resulted of these investigations have led to major changes to maritime practice. In the end, the International Ice Patrol was created in order to look out for and provide information on Icebergs that are found within the North Atlantic, giving ships that navigate through these dangerous waters with vital details. In order to avoid repeating fatal accidents, better safety regulations, enhanced the training of crew members, as well as stricter compliance with the lifeboat capacity requirements were set.

The effect of these investigations and investigations goes far beyond immediate effects. The sinking of the Titanic was an educational experience, and maritime security procedures continue to be in the shape of those lessons to this day. A commitment to readiness as well as vigilance and survival of humans on the water is proof of the long-lasting impact.

The investigation resulted in changes to the laws in addition to a sense of justice for the victim as well as their families. In the investigations, those who were responsible for the tragedy were held for the actions of those responsible in shedding light on shortcomings that led to the tragic incident. For the families who lost loved ones in that tragic night, the victims their testimonies as well as the investigation have provided closure as well as some measure of peace.

Changes in Safety Regulations

In the aftermath of the tragic sinking the Titanic the Titanic, there were significant changes regarding the law governing maritime safety. The deaths of many caused a rapid re-evaluation of the existing procedures as well as a commitment to avoid the same catastrophe from occurring in the future.

The entire world was shaken to the core when the extent of Titanic's vulnerability was revealed. The myth of an "unsinkable" ship was disproved The maritime industry realized the need to establish strict security standards, which put security of passengers as well as crew members first.

The world's governments and regulators were quick to intervene. As a direct reaction to the Titanic disaster, there was the an establishment of the International Convention for the Safety of Life at Sea (SOLAS). This landmark agreement set strict rules and regulations which all passenger ships were required to follow.

The need for a sufficient amount of lifeboats that could accommodate every passenger onboard was one of the main changes implemented. A glaring oversight in Titanic's lifeboat capacity being inadequate was an important factor in the death toll that was tragically high. In order to ensure that nobody was left in danger during emergencies, new rules required ships to come with lifeboats on board for each passenger onboard.

Additionally there was the SOLAS treaty established stringent security guidelines for the construction of ships and their design. The use of watertight compartments, increased strength of the hull, as well as improved stabilization criteria were among the main areas of concern. The goal of these measures is to increase the ship's resistance to shocks and maintain stability during unexpected incidents like grounding or collisions.

The introduction of the latest technologies for communication had a major role in enhancing safety at sea and also physical changes. Because of poor radio communication that other ships did missed the distress signals from Titanic. To ensure rapid and efficient distress signals as well as collaboration during times of emergency, SOLAS required the installation and operation of dependable wireless communications technology in all ships.

The training of crew members as well as exercises for safety saw a dramatic modification too. There was an overall lack of interest in disaster preparation prior to the Titanic sinking. The tragedy highlighted the urgency of necessity of a thorough and comprehensive training program as well as well-established protocols. SOLAS established regular drills in order to ensure crew members had a solid understanding of emergency procedures including evacuation techniques, as well as operating life-saving equipment.

The industry of maritime was profoundly affected by changes to security laws enacted through the tragedy of Titanic. Shipbuilders needed to alter their designs to comply with stringent requirements, while operators were faced with the issue in implementing and sustaining the latest safety guidelines. Because of the increasing attention to liability and safety in the insurance industry, they also had to examine their policies and the cost of their premiums.

You can see that the Titanic's sinking left an indelible mark which includes the actual tragedy as well as the dramatic changes that came because of it. Many lives were saved because of the security precautions put in after the tragedy. They are proof of humanity's strength and dedication to safeguarding the safety and well-being of those who traverse the huge oceans that surround the globe.

Memorializing the Tragedy

Sinking the Titanic was a catastrophe which shook the entire world, creating a permanent mark in our history as well as a profound sadness as a result. After the catastrophe there was a desire to remember the tragedy and pay homage to those people who were tragically killed.

Commemorative Memorials:

The Titanic and the passengers on board are remembered through the creation of memorials throughout the globe. These poignant memorials serve as symbol of rememberance and act as reminders of the massive human price.

The most famous of these is one of them is the Titanic Belfast It could be located in the town in which the ship was constructed. This iconic building not just is home to a museum that traces the history of Titanic, but it is also an ominous tribute to the individuals whose lives were forever altered on that fateful night. People who visit Titanic Belfast are able to explore the exhibitions, see objects, and gain greater understanding of events that led to the tragic Titanic's journey.

There are other memorials around the globe as well as those of the Titanic Belfast. These beautiful monuments, that extend across the globe, starting beginning with to the Titanic Memorial in Washington, D.C. and the Titanic Memorial Garden in Liverpool are a testimony to the resilience of humankind and serve as reminders of the long-lasting impact of the tragedy.

Memorial Services and Commemorative Events:

Celebrations and memorial ceremonies will be held to honor the lost lives and survivors' stories to make sure that the story of the Titanic remains. These events provide an opportunity to bring people together for reflection, to give their homage to those who suffered in the tragedy.

Each year, in the wake of the anniversary of Titanic's sinking, celebrations take place at various venues that bring people from diverse backgrounds together to reflect and celebrate the lives of those who have been tragically short-changed. The mournful events typically include musical performances, readings, as well as moments of silence in order to reflect on the tragedy and the Titanic's impact.

Artistic Expressions:

Many artistic pieces are being created as a way to show the magnitude of the Titanic disaster and its impact to humanity. The stories of the Titanic remain awe-inspiring to people around across the globe through writing and music, art as well as other types of art.

The event has been vividly depicted in films like "Titanic" and books like "A Night to Remember" written by Walter Lord, allowing audiences to be able to feel the emotion as well as the feelings of those who were aboard. These imaginative interpretations do more than provide entertainment, but also serves as a way of teaching and preserve the history of the Titanic to future generations.

Dear readers, the memory of Titanic is still felt through the monuments, celebrations and art works. They are a constant reminder of the tempo of our lives and the immense impact of human endeavour. They are a constant reminder to learn from the past, to cherish memories of those who have passed away and work towards the future that is more secure and more loving.

Let us remember the memory of the people who died and tell their stories when we walk on by these memorials. We can also participate in events that honor the deceased and interact with art works that were influenced by the Titanic. Their deaths should be a permanent reminder of the necessity of being cautious, safe, and an unwavering appreciation for the power of the ocean.

The moment the Ferry first Found Seven decades later incredible discovery was waiting for us in the vast depths of Atlantic Ocean, where the secrets of the depths had been buried for years. The discovery attracted the attention all over the world, and ignited curiosity about the tragedy of Titanic. A small group of adventurers began a risky voyage to discover the ship's final burial site, years after the devastating sinking.

The search for the Titanic was not an easy feat. It required a constant commitment as well as cutting-edge technology the support of a group of individuals who were driven by a keen fascination and the significance of history. The team was headed by prominent sea archaeologists, famous sea explorers and marine biologists were in charge of this challenging project.

The Dr. Robert Ballard, a well-known oceanographer who is well-known for his innovative deep-sea work is one of those driving factors in the creation of this mission. Dr. Ballard put together a team of experts, and began a quest which could alter the course of time with modern technology and a relentless determination.

A few years after the Titanic sink, progress in science has finally met the expectations of those hoping to discover the secrets of this ship. The latest sonar technology and remote operated vehicles (ROVs) equipped with high-resolution cameras as well as robotic arms were utilized to assist Dr. Ballard and his crew to search the depths of the ocean and search for the historical vessel's wreckage.

The Dr. Robert Ballard and his team discovered the first-ever finding of Titanic's remains on September 1st in 1985. They found the wreckage of the ship within the North Atlantic Ocean at a deep of 12,500 feet, thanks to the most advanced equipment as well as their unwavering determination. An important turning point in marine research and the understanding of one of the most famous tragedies came when the long-awaited glimpse of the Titanic and its wreckage, which was a mystery to researchers for seven years.

Investigating and studying the historical record, eyewitness accounts as well as the precise mapping of the Titanic's most recent position formed the basis for the task. The crew was adept at navigating the waters and meticulously searched the ocean's vast bottom while carefully plotting the search zone.

The days grew into weeks while the team persevered regardless of uncertainty in the depth sea's nature and its size. There were moments of doubt and anger, but their determination never wavered increased their determination. Initial signs of the Titanic began to emerge out of the shadows on an epochal day, as ROVs plunged deeper to the bottom.

It was an amazing and harrowing experience. The once magnificent ship stood in the waters it was an unsettling glimpse of the past. The ROVs efficiently navigated through the wreckage and took breath-taking photographs that permanently altered the way we see what the Titanic was resting at the time of its final voyage.

When the world learned about the amazing find an atmosphere of amazement and reflection swept through all the people. The Titanic's wreckage that were sheltered by the freezing depths of the sea, served as a tangible connection to the time of the past. It was a poignant reminding of the human costs of insanity as in addition to the tragic evening's lasting impacts.

The search for the Titanic has also triggered a renewed interest in marine archaeology. It also prompted more exploration and documentation visits to other sites of historical significance. The Titanic was an example of the ways in which technology and human creative thinking can help explore the depths of the sea and uncover a tangled part of our collective past.

It was an exciting, yet bittersweet experience for the dedicated team that discovered the Titanic. It was an incredible feat of human endeavour, but it was also an empathetic recall of the terrible incidents that occurred over a century ago and the loss of lives due to them.

Friends, the finding of the Titanic is a testament to the unending curiosity in the ever-expanding pursuit of knowledge, as well as the lasting tradition of a vessel which is a fascination throughout time. The Titanic serves as a poignant reminding us of the fragility of human life, and also an example of human achievement.

Join me as I journey into the ages of history and never forgetting the incredible incident that brought about the discovery of Titanic. Invigorated by the information acquired from the depths of the stories that lie under the seas We must continue to explore, uncover and protect the mystery of the world.

Chapter 5: Tragic Story Of Devastation Following

Beginning on Sunday 18th June through Tuesday, June 20, 2023 The following report was stated by BBC

Tuesday, 20th June 19.000 GMT, 2023

In a race to beat the clock the search teams are searching the depths of the ocean for the submersible which went missing in a dive near the world-class shipwreck of the Titanic. The tiny tourist boat with five persons on board was lost for about an hour and 45 mins in its dive, on Sunday.

Based on information supplied from the US Coast Guard, the sub was left with about 40 hours left of oxygen on Tuesday, at 13:00 Eastern Standard Time (18:00 BST). The search for the submarine became greater urgency as a result of the information. However, despite the fact that they extended their search to deeper waters within mid-sized waters of Atlantic The submarine that was missing could not be found.

British businessman Hamish Harding, British-Pakistani businessman Shahzada Dawood and his son Suleman, French adventurer Paul-Henry Nargeolet, as well as Stockton Rush, the CEO of OceanGate who was the company that was responsible for the diving, were among the five persons who were on the ship that was tragically lost.

The news briefing on Tuesday afternoon was held by Captain Jamie Frederick of the US Coast Guard He declared that even though teams of searchers were at work non-stop however, they have not discovered something. The hunt, as per Capt. Frederick the search proved to be "very complex," covering a vast area.

The US as well as Canadian agencies, deep-sea commercial firms, as well as government agencies collaborated on the rescue efforts. Sonar buoys, a submarine as well as military aircrafts were utilized, along in conjunction with a variety of private vessels. The search has been assisted with Deep Energy, a commercial pipe-laying vessel equipped with submersibles that are remote.

David Mearns, a well-known oceanographer, shipwreck hunter and marine biologist said he was confident that Deep Energy's capability to investigate the 3,800m (12,500 feet) of the Titanic wreckage to find the submarine that was missing. Mearns was in a close connection to the Mr. Harding and Mr. Nargeolet Two of the people who were aboard the. The 58-year old man. Harding is a renowned adventurer who's broken the world record three times and has even went into space. The man recently spoke out of his pride to have been a participant in the project. A former French Navy diver and officer the late Mr. Nargeolet, 77, is now in charge of the Titanic wreck's recovery firm's director of research in the ocean.

Although the Titanic is situated about 435 miles (700km) to the south from St John's, Newfoundland, located in Canada the search and rescue effort is coordinated by Boston,

Massachusetts. Boston, Massachusetts, in the United States.

According to the US Coast Guard reported that Deep Energy and the Polar Prince the ship that provided support that was part of the Sunday tourism mission are still exploring the sea's surface. On Tuesday an Canadian P3 Aurora aircraft was conducting sonar surveys over a territory which covers over 10,000 sq miles (26,900 square kilometers).

The French minister of the sea has helped in the search efforts through the diverting of the Atalante ship, which was fitted with a subsea robotic.

OceanGate is the operator of the Titan The Titan, the submarine that has gone missing. It's crucial to know that CBS reporter David Pogue visited the Titanic wreck earlier this year when he was traveling aboard the Titan. As per Pogue Short text messages can be exchanged and received by the support ship and sub, while being immediately over each other. Submarine radios as well as GPS transmission, however cannot be achieved. In addition, because of the insufficient sunlight penetration, visibility quickly drops below the water's surface.

According to the OceanGate website, the company has three submersibles, with Titan as the one that is able to dive deep enough to recover debris from the Titanic debris. According to OceanGate's site, Titan's deepest dive depth of 13,100 feet. the weight is more than 23,000 pounds (10,432 kilograms). Every ticket on the 8-day cruise cost $250,000 (PS195,000) and also includes diving to the depth of 3,800 meters Titanic wreck.

He. Harding posted on social media saying that the mission would likely to be the last manned journey towards the Titanic in 2023, due it was a bad weather. Then, he wrote, "A weather window has just opened up, and we are going to attempt a dive tomorrow."

OceanGate Later, the company confirmed that one of its submersible exploration vehicles wasn't able to talk with it.

OceanGate's main focus is its crew members on the submersible as well as their families. They expressed their gratitude for the enormous assistance they that they received from various government agencies as well as deep-sea companies in efforts to reconnect to the submarine.

The expedition is presented by the company as an unique chance to escape the ordinary daily life to discover something amazing. Starting at St. John's in Newfoundland every full dive up towards the wreck, including the climb and descent is said to take around 8 hours. On OceanGate's web site an ongoing dive as well as two planned expeditions in June 2024 are in the planning stage.

The Titanic has been a fascination for the entire world since her tragic sinking in the first of her voyages to Southampton towards New York in 1912. After its first discovery in 1985 2200 passengers and staff members are being investigated thoroughly, and more than 1,500 people have been killed. The tragic incident was much more urgent and uncertain because of the need to recover the submersible.

Enormous Search Efforts

The need to locate the submarine that was missing grew over these past days, prompting the world's search and rescue efforts to ramp up. On Sunday, at 11:47 the last communication of the submarine with the mothership that is the Polar Prince, took place. Submersibles were only guided via text messages from the ship's surface since there wasn't any GPS submerged.

The teams of searchers employed a range of equipment to explore the surroundings as well as the sea bottom. When planes flew by the area that was searched the remote operated vehicle was dispatched to investigate the deepest parts. An French ship also assisted in the search, by setting off its own remote-controlled vehicle. This Magellan crew, who already plotted where to find the

Titanic wreckage, was currently headed to offer the aid of the crew.

Families and relatives of those who were aboard the missing sailing vessel had moments of hope in the hunt. Sonar sensors detected loud noises in the ocean on Tuesday and Wednesday, within the extensive search zone. The origins of these sounds, but, remain a mystery. The official US government document that provides details on the hunt claims that the sounds first surfaced on the Tuesday that lasted 30 minutes and then returned 4 hours later. Mauger who was involved of the hunt, said that he wasn't sure if these sounds were connected to the location of the submersible located on the sea floor.

It is believed that the US Navy contributed their expertise in analyzing the audio signals of the sound and other data from acoustics discovered as part of the search for the purpose of determining what caused the noise. The sounds are most likely to be related to natural phenomenon or a sound produced by another ship or vessels participating in the search, an Navy official speaking to CNN revealed. Officials made it clear that there did not appear to be any link between the sound results as well as the actual location of the submersible at sea.

In its underwater acoustic hearing system that was in operation, this US Navy had access to numerous sensors which could listen to the sounds from the explosion. It was noted by the source that there was no significant progress been made on locating the submarine that was lost due to the explosion.

The international teams came in tandem in the course of the rescue and search operations progressed in search of evidence of the ship's disappearance. The race against time was on with everyone's attention determined to find the submarine that was missing and its crew.

The 5 Billionaires Who Lost Life Following A Catastrophic Explosion of Submersible.

Based on information collected through various resources, this is the information we have on the billionaires of five who lived in the submersible

Shahzada Dawood:

A businessman Shahzada Dawood, a British-born Pakistani who served as vice-chairman of Karachi in Pakistan. Engro Corporation. Dawood was from one of the wealthiest family of entrepreneurs within Pakistan. He specialized in technology as well as renewable energy. Dawood was born in Rawalpindi, Pakistan, on the 12th of February, 1975 was a law student in Buckingham University before going on to complete his master's degree in international textile marketing. Dawood was honored when the World Economic Forum named him as a Young Global Leader in 2012. Shahzada Dawood was accompanied by his son, 19 years old Suleman Dawood, on the Titan submersible.

Suleman Dawood:

Suleman Dawood, Shahzada Dawood's daughter, who was 19 when he studied in Glasgow's business school, the University of Strathclyde. Suleman Dawood shared the same passion for adventure and exploration that his father did. Suleman was identified as a lover in science-fiction, a competitive volleyball player and Rubik's cube enthusiast. In the moment of the incident, he was completed his academic year.

Paul-Henri Nargeolet:

French explorationist Paul-Henri Nargeolet, 77, was considered to be an expert regarding the Titanic. He was a part of RMS Titanic, an American company that holds the salvage rights of the vessel, and was director of underwater research. Nargeolet is often referred to for his role as "Titanic's Greatest Explorer," was the leader of six expeditions to the site of the Titanic's sinking. He was a captain within the French Navy and also had an extensive experience of miningsweeping and deep sea diving.

Stockton Rush:

OceanGate The organization that is responsible for running the Titan submersible, was established by Stockton Rush. Rush was the pilot of the submarine, was a pilot with experience in aviation. He was awarded his DC-8 Type/Captain's certificate in the United Airlines Jet Training Institute in 1981, at 19 years old, and was the tiniest jet transport pilot anywhere in the world. Rush was an integral part of the process to the creation of OceanGate with the goal to explore and protect our oceans.

Hamish Harding:

British Entrepreneur as well as Action Aviation chairman Hamish Harding was famous for his bold ventures. The company he ran was focused on selling planes to business leaders from around the world, executive, and famous people in the entertainment and sports sectors. According to The British news, Harding was referred to as a billionaire. He was previously a participant on the "One

More Orbit" flight mission that was the most efficient circumnavigation of the Earth through the air. On social media, he posted in excitement regarding the voyage of a submersible on the Titanic.

Five individuals who were driven by a common spirit of curiosity and adventure and exploration, tragically perished in the course of submersible travel. The families of the deceased and their loved ones grieved for the loss of these authentic explorers, highlighting their devotion to knowledge and exploration into the unexplored.

The Catastrophic Implosion.

22 June 2023 (Reuters) 22 June 2023 (Reuters) U.S. Coast Guard reported the incident as a "catastrophic implosion" that claimed the lives of five aboard, concluding the five-day long international search for the submersible deep in the sea Titan. In the early hours of Thursday an underwater robotic vehicle launching from an Canadian ship discovered the Titan submarine's debris field,

which was 1600 feet (488 meters) just off the bow of the Titanic in the distant North Atlantic. The shocking announcement was made at the press conference of U.S. Coast Guard Rear Admiral John Mauger, bringing an ending to the lengthy hunt for the missing.

Soundscapes from the Deep

Scientists aimed to determine precisely when the Titan was struck by its fateful crash and the inquiry into the cause of the explosion began. The sonar buoys had been placed in place for more than three days, without finding any loud and violent sound related to an explosion, the proximity of the debris field to the shipwreck as well as the time of Titan's last message suggested the incident occurred close to the conclusion of the descent on Sunday. After the submersible's communication was cut off and it was discovered that the U.S. Navy found an anomaly which was probably due to an implosion or explosion near to the submarine's position. The top-secret method that was used to detect adversary submarine picked up the sounds.

Interestingly, the renowned producer in the film "Titanic" James Cameron, who had also personal adventures with the wreckage, was informed about the results of the acoustic tests the following day. Cameron broke the devastating news and mourned at the passing of fellow crew members and inform them that the sub has exploded and is now broken up floating on the ocean the floor.

The Tragic Fate of the Explorers

In the days prior to the Coast Guard's news announcement, OceanGate Expeditions, the American company responsible for overseeing the Titan has issued an announcement that stated that no one of the five people in the submarine had been able to survive. Captain of the Titan, Stockton Rush, the founder and chief executive officer of OceanGate is among the victims. British billionaire Hamish Harding, Pakistani-born entrepreneur Shahzada Dawood, Dawood's son Suleman aged 19 as well as renowned French oceanographer Paul-Henri Nargeolet were among the others who were killed. Their families as well as the firm were deeply affected at losing these persons as true oceanographers who had a burning desire to safeguard the seas around the globe.

The Search and Challenges Ahead

To find the Titan the search teams and staff from United States, Canada, France as well as Britain have spent days flying across and sailing through huge expanses of water. The global coverage of the hunt obliterated the aftermath of an even bigger maritime tragedy which involved a boat carrying migrant migrants in the waters off Greece.

Remotely operated robots were deployed following the initial search in order to collect information from the field of debris. Recovery of the injured' remains was very difficult because of what happened in the crash as well as the depths of the crash. Coast Guard Rear Admiral John Mauger stated that the ships and personnel would start to withdraw from the site in the coming 24 hours, indicating the conclusion of the hunt.

The Unfathomable Depths and Colossal Forces

The devastating collapse of Titan could be attributable to the massive forces that are at work within the deep sea. Pressures reach 4000 pounds for every square inch almost 140 times that of the pressure in the sea at depths equivalent to the top of a 150-story building. Constructions built for at these depths will have to endure extreme conditions, even with the most advanced design and construction. The harsh conditions and the intense pressure of the sea below may force submersibles to the force of crushing that is greater than the limits of their structure.

Paying Tribute to the Fallen Explorers

The entire world is grieving due to the tragic incident which involved the Titan submersible's horrific explosion in it's dive into the Titanic. Stockton Rush, Hamish Harding, Shahzada and Suleman Dawood along with Paul-Henri Nagreolet died in a sudden manner, and left behind grieving relatives, friends and colleagues. After this tragic event since the tragedy, a flood of heartfelt messages have come into the world to honor the brave men and women who sacrificed their lives for the exploration of oceans and conservation.

The world has seen an flood of support for the death of these courageous individuals. When the news broke celebrities expressed their sadness and praised the life of those who died. Presidents, CEOs, moguls, adventurers, and even the president of the United States all wrote condolence and letters of support to the family members of those who lost their lives. To pay tribute to the explorers with their unrelenting passion and commitment for the safety of the oceans of the world, OceanGate Expeditions has established an endowment fund that will promote research and safety in the ocean.

Recognizing True Explorers

The Titan submersible's operator OceanGate Expeditions, has recognized guests for being "true explorers who shared a distinct spirit of adventure and a deep passion for exploring and protecting the world's oceans." Their lives were characterized by an ongoing pursuit of knowledge and understanding. Their loss tragically been a permanent mark upon the world of exploration as well as over the years.

Remembering Stockton Rush:

A victim Stockton Rush, the CEO of OceanGate Expeditions, is remembered for his visionary leadership that inspired people who were around him. We will be forever thankful for his commitment to exploring the oceans and his major contributions to this area. The joy and love the people who he encountered are cherished by his family, friends and colleagues. His legacy will be the basis for inspiration in years to come.

Honoring Hamish Harding:

British famous explorationist Hamish Harding was known as a loving father and mentor. He was also a persona, and a legendary figure. Harding inspired people to push the boundaries of their lives by leading an unending exploration and curiosity. His family grieves over the loss of a man with a great personality who was a true believer in his pursuits however they can take peace in the fact that he did the things he was passionate about.

Paying Tribute to Shahzada and Suleman Dawood:

The businessman Shahzada Dawood, who was born in Pakistan as was his son Suleman both died during the Titan submerged accident. Their grief-stricken family members confirmed their deaths and thanked all those who helped in the search. Suleman's bright career as a business school first-year pupil in Strathclyde University and Shahzada Dawood's notable achievements as vice chair in the company Engro Corporation both leave a lasting impression. Family as well as their friends and whole community offer their heartfelt sympathy and sorrow over their tragic loss.

Remembering Paul-Henri Nargeolet:

Paul-Henri Nargeolet, a renowned professional in deep-sea research, dedicated a significant part of his time resolve the problems of Titanic. He was a part of the RMS Titanic for many years and was a key part of many diving expeditions to the wreck. There, he was responsible for the retrieval from hundreds of pieces. The unrivaled depth of his knowledge and passion for exploring left an indelible impression on the marine sector. His loss Nargeolet is felt deeply by his family, friends and all the members of the exploration community.

Expressing Condolences and Support:

The messages of condolence and solidarity have flowed through from across the globe to mourn the tragedy. It is reported that the

White House acknowledged the traumatic event that families and their family members went through, and offered its condolences to the families. The British families that have been devastated by this tragedy receive a lot of help of government officials from the UK government. Additional Pakistani officials from the government, as well as friends and family members from those in the Dawood family have also sent condolence notes that highlight the impact Shahzada as well as Suleman Dawood had on their neighbourhood and on the wider world.

Tributes to Exploration Community: Tributes from Exploration Community:

Paul-Henri Nargeolet and Hamish Harding were trustees for the Explorers Club, which has expressed sorrow over the passing of their respective trustees. They were acknowledged as pioneers, who had dedicated their lives to vital studies and continuous research. Their work and dedication to exploring new ideas will be remembered.

Chapter 6: Titanic Short History

The Titanic was an British luxury ocean liner, which suffered a tragic sinking during its inaugural journey in 1912. The building of the Titanic began on the 31st of March 1909 at the Harland and Wolff shipyard in Belfast, Northern Ireland. It took three years to construct the enormous ship. It was built to be the biggest and most elegant passenger vessel of its period. The Titanic was 882 feet (269 meters) in length, and carried an average gross weight of 46,000 tonnes. It was equipped with lavish amenities that included swimming pools Turkish baths, a gym and squash court as well as lavish first-class lodgings.

On the 10th of April, 1912 on April 10, 1912, the Titanic embarked on the first voyage of its kind starting from Southampton, England, bound to New York City. The ship carried around 2224 people, including crew members and passengers. The trip was widely covered because of the Titanic's massive grandeur and luxury.

The night of April 14th, 1912, as it sailed through the North Atlantic Ocean, the Titanic was struck by an iceberg approximately 11:40 p.m. The iceberg was a major cause of damages to the ship's wooden interior, puncturing numerous compartments as well as causing floods.

The flooding grew worse, and it was evident that the Titanic was at risk of sinking. The distress signals were broadcast to nearby ships. Several such as those of the RMS Carpathia, responded to the request for assistance. But, because of a lack of lifeboats, and insufficient evacuation protocols, more than 1500 people died in the tragedy.

The sinking of Titanic caused shock to the entire world, and prompted important changes in the safety of ships. Inquiries and investigations were carried out to identify the reasons for the sinking as well as the lessons to be learned from this tragedy. The British as well as the American government held separate investigations looking into matters such as the absence of lifeboats as well as the lack of safety standards as well as the conduct that the crew.

The whereabouts of Titanic's wreckage was unanswered. In 1985, an American-French team under the direction of the Dr. Robert Ballard discovered the remains of the vessel at around 12,500 feet (3,800 meters) in the North Atlantic. The find shed light on the state of the ship and further helped in understanding the events that led to the sinking.

Through the years, numerous salvage efforts were conducted in order to salvage artifacts from the wreckage area. Some tens of thousands of objects, including private belongings, china as well as sections of the ship have been recovered and saved. They have given valuable information about the living conditions aboard the Titanic and are displayed in museums all over the world.

The Titanic's story Titanic is now a recurrent representation of human drama and strength. The Titanic has inspired a variety of pieces of literature, music and art in addition to memorial sites that honor the dead. Its sinking Titanic is still a source of fascination to the imagination of people everywhere, and serves as a reminder for the importance of enhancing safety procedures as well as the awareness that human beings are vulnerable.

The stories of individual people who were passengers or crew members on the Titanic are equally memorable. Certain individuals displayed bravery and selflessness in the course of evacuation. Other including the musicians who performed music until the vessel sank have been praised for their bravery to face the threat of disaster.

Sinking the Titanic is celebrated every year on the 15th of April, which is when the ship was sunk. There are many memorials and events that are held throughout the world to honor the fallen and honour the memory of their loved ones. Important anniversaries, like the centennial year in 2012 usually receive special recognition and attention.

The tale of the Titanic is warning tale to remind the people of the cost of egoism and the importance of taking safety into consideration in all marine activities. The Titanic story continues to have an impression on general public's consciousness, and has a profound impact on the way we conduct business and establishing safety standards.

The sinking of Titanic caused a significant effect on maritime history as well as safety rules. After the tragedy, extensive investigation was conducted to discover the reasons for the disaster and what lessons could be learned. The investigations led to major modifications in the shipbuilding process as well as safety standards.

One of the most significant result was the formation of the International Ice Patrol. The organization was established to keep track of icebergs that were forming in the North Atlantic and provide early alerts to ships operating within the region to ensure more secure navigation.

In addition to that, also, the International Convention for the Safety of Life at Sea (SOLAS) was adopted in 1914. The international treaty imposed stricter security measures for ships which included the need for enough lifeboats for everyone on the ship and mandatory lifeboat exercises, enhanced communication and communications systems, as well as adopting the "women and children first" evacuation plan.

The legacy of Titanic's voyage also spurred advances in technology. Submarines as well as remote operated vehicle (ROVs) were created for exploration of the depths the sea and to examine the site of the wreck. The advancements in technology allowed historians and scientists to develop more knowledge of what led to the sinking, as well as the state of the ship. Through the decades, the story of the Titanic was immortalized through different kinds of media. Many books, documentaries as well as films have been created that have captured the tragic event and human tales associated to the tragedy. James Cameron's film "Titanic" became a global phenomenon, sparking enthusiasm for the tragedy and introducing it to an younger generation.

The wreckage of Titanic is a poignant memorial to the lost lives and the tragic events that transpired on that night of calamity. There have been efforts to conserve the site and shield the site from further degradation. But, questions have been expressed about the effects on salvage and tourism operations on the structure of the wreckage.

Recently there has been discussion concerning the possibility of creating a protected maritime heritage area around the Titanic's wreckage, which would ensure the preservation of its remains for generations to come as well as paying tribute to the people who lost their lives.

The tale of the Titanic is still resonating as a testimony to humanity's determination, struggle, and the unstoppable determination of the human spirit to survive. The Titanic is warning tale to remind our minds of the dangers of human endeavours as well as the importance of putting safety first even in the midst of technological developments.

Although the Titanic was a victim of a terrible fate and was lost to history, the Titanic's story will be written in the history books and will remind us to take lessons from the past, and to strive for a better and safer safe future in the field of transportation and exploration in the maritime sector.

The tragedy of Titanic's voyage went far past safety guidelines and representations. The Titanic left an irresistible mark upon the lives of survivors and loved ones of the victims. They, who are often described as "Titanic's Unsinkable," faced major psychological and emotional challenges in the aftermath of this traumatic incident.

A lot of survivors devoted their lives in honoring the memory of victims and promoting improved security on the seas. They narrated their personal stories via memoirs, interviews and public speaking events to ensure that the lessons learnt from the Titanic's tragic loss did not go unnoticed.

The sinking of Titanic also brought about a wide range of economic implications. White Star Line, the company that owned and operated White Star Line, the owner of the ship was battling legal disputes for a long time as well as compensation claims from family members of the deceased. The catastrophe led to a drop in confidence among passengers, which led to less demand for transatlantic flights for a certain duration of.

The shipping industry was further improved on the ship's design and safety features. The focus shifted towards enhancing compartmentalization, strengthening hulls, implementing advanced communication systems, and refining evacuation procedures. Lessons learned from Titanic's sinking have shaped the modern-day maritime industry and safety standards.

Through the years, numerous trips have explored the wreckage of the Titanic, recording pictures of high-resolution and performing investigations in science. The explorations have exposed that the ship is slowly degrading vessel due to the extreme underwater conditions and the presence of deep-sea creatures. Discussions are in progress regarding the balance between preserving the wreckage site while also allowing an ethical exploration process and scientific research.

In the year 2020 the site of the Titanic's wreck the Titanic was declared an internationally-protected underwater cultural heritage area under the United Nations Educational, Scientific and Cultural Organization (UNESCO). The designation is intended to protect the area and stop unauthorized salvage activities or affecting the wreckage of the ship.

The impact of the Titanic remains awe-inspiring to people around the world with exhibits and museums dedicated to the preservation of its story. The visitors can visit detailed replicas, look at artifacts found from the wreckage as well as learn about the personal tales of those that were on board.

Beyond its cultural and historical effects beyond the impact on culture and history, the Titanic has been an emblem of strength and perseverance of humankind in the facing of challenges. The Titanic serves as a warning that even the biggest and almost invincible endeavors may be slowed down by the forces of natural forces.

The tale of the Titanic is a constant reminder to humanity's spirit as well as how important it is to strive for security, kindness and remembering. It is still able to stir up intense emotions, motivate new research and spur the continuous effort to increase the safety of ships around the world.

The recent advances in science and technology provide new ways for researchers to investigate the Titanic and the significance of its history. Researchers have employed sophisticated imaging methods including sonar scanning and 3D mapping to produce detailed models of the vessel as well as its debris. These reconstructions give valuable insights on the structural integrity the ship and aid in unravelling the mystery of the ship's sinking.

Alongside scientific research and exploration, Titanic's history has inspired other acts of remembrance and commemoration. The memorial services take place each year on the 15th April to commemorate the loss of lives by the tragedy. World-wide, people come together to pay respects and think about the devastating impact of the tragedy.

The legacy of the Titanic has also prompted charitable efforts. A variety of charitable organisations and initiatives were created in honor of those who lost their lives, and aim to help causes that are that concern maritime safety as well as education and the relief of natural disasters.

The Titanic's epic tale remains a magnet for the imagination of film makers, writers and even artists. The classic tale of sacrifice, love and human fragility has been made into numerous stages, films and books, keeping the tale alive in pop media.

Technology is constantly evolving, and it is being discussed possibilities for the further exploration of the Titanic. Many are suggesting using autonomous underwater vehicles (AUVs) and robotics in order to explore the wreckage further as well as better comprehend the reasons that led to its sinking.

In spite of the passing of time The Titanic is a constant emblem of resilience and loss. Its history is a constant reminder that, even in the midst of adversity, our spirit is resilient and lessons are to be taken away. The tale of the Titanic is still able to captivate and delight generations to come, instilling admiration for the tales of those who were aboard and also the significance of safety preservation and memory of maritime heritage.

The Titanic was built mainly from steel, the most popular material for the shipbuilding industry during that time. The structure of the Titanic was comprised of two bottoms and 16 compartments that were watertight, intended to offer stability and increase the buoyancy. The steel plates which formed part of the outside vessel were joined with rivets to create an extremely sturdy construction.

The steel that was used to construct the Titanic was of a particular type called mild steel that offered a great balance of workability and strength. This kind of steel was extensively utilized in ship construction due to its toughness and its resistance to corrosion.

The plates of steel used to construct the Titanic's wooden hull were about 1 inch (2.5 centimeters) in thickness towards the bottom of the ship, but diminished in size towards the top of the vessel. The total weight of the ship was approximately 46,000 tons which makes it among the biggest and largest ships of the time.

Although the steel structure provided substantial strength to Titanic however, the tragic event highlighted its vulnerability in the event of hitting an glacier. The collision triggered the steel plates to give way and the seams that were riveted to break which led to the bursting of the compartments, and eventually sinking the ship.

Apart from steel, other elements were utilized in the design of the Titanic. The interiors were decorated with lavish and extravagant decorations, which included items like marble, wood and even glass. The magnificent staircase, which was an important feature of Titanic built with wood paneling, the wrought iron of which was used, as well as intricate sculptures. The walls of first-class public areas were covered by rich wood paneling as were the floors, which were lined with a luxurious carpet.

The luxurious cabins had elegant woodwork, soft fabric, and exquisite furniture. Many of the most luxurious cabins were decorated with mahogany, walnut, or satinwood-like finishes. The cabins of the second and third class were more basic in appearance, featuring less expensive furniture and materials.

In the vessel it was awash with ports and windows made from glass, allowing sunlight to enter the interior areas. Glass used for windows was usually made of top quality and ensured the clarity and strength.

The Titanic was also equipped with a broad assortment of equipment and facilities. There were several dining options on board as well as a café, smoking room, a library and even a gym. The rooms were decorated by combining substances like leather, wood as well as fabric upholstery.

The dining rooms were outfitted with exquisite chairs and tables, usually constructed of solid wood. Crystal glassware, fine china as well as silver cutlery was served for meals, adding to the overall elegance and splendor of the ship.

The engineering section of the Titanic there were a variety of electrical and mechanical components were put in place. They included big generators, boilers, engines as well as electrical systems. The machines were made from a mix of metals like iron, steel, and brass.

The building of the Titanic comprised a broad range of different materials. It combined the strength of steel to construct its structure, along with the elegance of glass, wood as well as other luxurious materials to create its interior areas. The result was the Titanic as a vessel which was not just sturdy but also beautiful, and comfortable for the passengers.

The building of the Titanic was the work by a multitude of skilled and experienced workers as well as artisans. The ship was constructed in Harland and Wolff, a Harland and Wolff shipyard in Belfast, Northern Ireland, in which a large number of people took their time assembling the ship's various components.

The steel that was used for the building was cut and formed by experienced metalworkers who precisely cut, riveted and joined the steel plates to form the huge structure of the vessel's hull. Riveting in particular was a time-consuming process that required warming the rivets until they reached a temperature of red hot, and pressing them down in order to form a strong and waterproof seal.

Carpenters and woodworkers were key to creating the lavish interiors on the Titanic. They expertly shaped and cut the paneling of wood or molding and furniture by creating elaborate design and stunning finish. The craftsmen paid close care to each and every little detail and ensured that their wooden work was of the highest standard in terms of craftsmanship and quality. Glassworkers created portsholes, windows, as well as decorative glass components across the entire ship. They employed techniques like cutting shape, polishing, and shaping for the creation of clear as well as decorative glass designs that decorated the Titanic's inside as well as its outside.

Artists and craftsmen who were skilled in different materials like brass, marble, and fabrics. They created stunning fittings made from marble and fittings made of polished brass, as well as upholstered furniture that added the appearance of grandiosity and elegance to the vessel's appearance.

The building of Titanic was a huge task that demanded the collaboration of many skilled artisans and crafters. Their combined expertise and attention to detail helped to the design of a vessel which was not just well-built but also beautiful and lavish.

The work of these artisans and their workers helped bring the idea that was the Titanic to life, transforming it into an edifice of water which sought to redefine sophistication and luxury when it came to traveling by sea. But, the tragedy of the Titanic can serve as a warning that the best achievements of engineering and craft could be exposed to unexpected events and elements of nature.

Chapter 7: Titanic Submarine

Rear Admiral John Mauger of the US Coast Guard declared on Thursday that the Titanic submarine which went missing on Sunday along with five other passengers aboard suffered an "catastrophic implosion," killing the entire crew. According to Mauger the remotely-operated vehicle located that Titan's tail cone approximately 1600 feet off the ship's bow.

The passengers included: Stockton Rush, the director of tour company OceanGate Expeditions, along with Hamish Harding, Paul-Henri nargeolet, Shahzada Dawood and his son Suleman Dawood, perished in the ship. Submersibles were descending to examine the wreckage of the luxury liner that was about 13,000 feet beneath sea level, and was approximately 900 miles to the from Cape Cod.

The announcement regarding the Titan submersible's catastrophic explosion, as per James Cameron, director of the cult 1997 movie "Titanic," "certainly wasn't a surprise."

Cameron himself, who personally dived 33 times to the Titan's wreckage, revealed to the CNN's Anderson Cooper that after learning about the Titan incident in the morning on Monday Cameron immediately made contact with his submerged group of a small members and was informed in less than a half hour that the submersible was simultaneously losing communication and track.

On Thursday, he said "The only scenario I could think of in my mind that could account for that was an implosion." Another system that has its own pressure vessel as well as power source for batteries was damaged by a shockwave.

According to a top Navy official According to a senior Navy official, the US Navy discovered an implosion-like audio signature on Sunday, in the area around the area where Titan was located. Titan submersible was scuba diving in the North Atlantic when it lost contact with the support vessel.

The Navy quickly informed the officers who are in charge of the hunt operation on the ground, the official stated on Thursday. The official added this helped focus the hunt.

The official evaluated the sound of the explosion as "not definitive," however it was determined that the search and rescue effort to locate the submersible continued.

James Cameron, who directed the successful 1997 film "Titanic" and has made 33 dives into the wreckage of the Titan, has said that he noticed several similarities between Titan tragedy as well as the sinking of the legendary ship that it was to be bound for.

"I'm struck by the similarity of the Titanic disaster itself, where the captain was repeatedly warned about ice ahead of his ship and yet steamed at full speed into an ice field on a moonless night and many people died as a result," Cameron reported to ABC News Thursday. Cameron added "And with a very similar tragedy where warnings went unheeded to take place at the same exact site with all the diving that's going on all around the world I think it's just astonishing. It's really quite surreal."

The missing Titanic Submarine Regular Updates. Reports have confirmed that the Titan submarine, which is operated through OceanGate Expeditions, has exploded within the Atlantic Ocean. The submarine set off for an exploration trip to study the Titanic debris near the shores of Newfoundland on the 18th of June But two hours later, the vessel lost contact. The lavish trip included an acknowledged Titanic specialist, a record holder explorer, two members from one of the richest families in Pakistan, as well as the CEO of the company. The 18th June was a Sunday 18 June, the US Coast Guard joined forces together with deep-water specialists from Canada and the UK as well as France in a hunt operation to locate the Titan submarine. This triggered an international rescue effort. But, the US Coast Guard announced yesterday that no one was rescued.

Capt. Mark Martin, a salvage master and deep-submergence captain, told reporters on Thursday that, if equipped appropriately, just a single ship as well as remote-controlled vessels in the ocean's bottom could definitely be able to collect the Titan submersible's remains. Martin declared during an interview with CNN's Jake Tapper that the ship requires a crane equipped with cable capable of reaching an underwater depth of 4,000 meters (about 2.5 miles) this is a common feature with many of the vessels that are used for offshore construction of oil and gas.

A couple of remotely operated vehicles, also known as ROVs are already vital in the hunt to find Titan's remains, could be requested by the team's recovery efforts, the captain stated. ROVs are ROVs are massive, durable equipment that could be operated by remote control.

Was it?

The news reports reveal that the Titan submarine, which is operated through OceanGate Expeditions, has exploded within the Atlantic Ocean. The submarine set off for an expedition to look into the Titanic debris that was discovered off the coast of Newfoundland on the 18th of June however, two hours later the vessel lost contact. This lavish excursion was led by an acknowledged Titanic expert and a world-record-holding researcher, two of one of the richest Pakistani families, as well as the CEO of the company. The 18th June was a Sunday on the 18th of June, the US Coast Guard joined forces with deep-water experts from Canada as well as the UK and France to begin a search of the Titan submarine. The search triggered an international rescue effort. However, yesterday it was announced that officials from the US Coast Guard said the catastrophic deep-water collapse had left no survivors.

What did Titan research cost? The most extensive searching for the lost Titan submersible will cost millions of dollars as per experts. There was a team of experts from the US Coast Guard, the Canadian Coast Guard, the US Navy, as well as other private and government agencies, searched a territory which was hundreds of miles in length and twice as large as Connecticut as well as in water which were 2 and two-and-a-half mile (4 km) deep.

According to the naval historian Norman Polmar, there are none of the previous ocean researches which can be considered comparable particularly with the present presence of so many countries as well as for-profit companies.

The entire aircraft costs tens of thousands dollars an hour to run as per the Government Accountability Office. In addition, C-130 Hercules as well as jet powered P-8 Poseidon subhunters, turboprop P-3 Orion.

Who were among the casualties of the explosion? The casualties of the implosion included Oceangate Chief Executive Officer and Titan pilot Stockton Rush, Shahzada Dawood and his son Suleman Dawood, a well-known Pakistani family. British aventurer Hamish Harding Hamish Harding, as well as Titanic expert Paul-Henri Nagreolet.

The liability waivers that passengers signed of a submersible that was which was lost at sea in diving into the Titanic wreck could not safeguard owners of the vessel from legal action brought by victims' family members. They have paid up to $250,000 per person for a trip from 12,500 to (3,810 metres) beneath the sea surface may have executed the liability waivers. But, Reuters cited legal experts to point out that these documents don't always have the same and cannot be guaranteed.

It's not uncommon that judges will reject cases when there is proof of negligent conduct or dangerous situations that weren't fully identified.

What happened to the Titan submersible vanish? The Titan submersible sank into the ocean, where it was completely lost within 45 and an hour minutes later.

The Titan ship was reported to be overdue approximately 435 miles (700 kilometers) to the south from St. John's, Newfoundland.

Titan Titan was launched by an icebreaker which was commissioned by OceanGate and previously owned under the Canadian Coast Guard.

The Titan has transported a number of individuals and the Submersible Craft to its North Atlantic wreck site, in which the Titan has been diving multiple times.

Bodies may not get recovered

Titan submersible that was undiscovered for four days. and the US Coastal Guard found its debris in the night of Thursday at about 1,600 feet away from the Titanic's wreckage. The five passengers are declared dead as they were a members of the search. The bodies of the deceased won't be found, but the coast guard has been conducting a search operations. amish Harding, Paul-Henri Nargeolet, Shahzada Dawood and his son Suleman Dawood, and Stockton Rush who is the CEO of OceanGate arrived in Newfoundland to look into the wreckage of the Titanic ship.

What are the ways OceanGate will protect it from harm?

OceanGate may seek to protect itself from harm by bringing an "limitation of liability" lawsuit under maritime law which allows the owners of a vessel who are the victims of an accident request the federal court to restrict damages up to the present worth that the boat. Because the Titan was destroyed, the value could be the case.

However, OceanGate will have to show that it was unaware of possible defects in the submersible, and it would have to carry the burden of proof that legal experts say is an extremely difficult task to complete.

If OceanGate failed in such a situation the families could be free to bring claims for negligence or wrongful deaths.

A different maritime law, called The Death on the High Seas Act provides for those who are financially dependent upon someone who passed away due to a maritime accident claim only the amount of future earnings they might have had.

What OceanGate did they know about the safety of the vessel and the information that passengers received about it will be the most important questions to be asked during the investigation.

The submersible in the deep-sea Titan which came to an unsettling conclusion on Thursday was operated with a video game controller. Some old footage has surfaced on the web revealing how the luxury cruise, with a cost of approximately 2 crores, was run with an F710 controller which connects wirelessly to gaming consoles as well as PCs.

Chapter 8: Hamish Harding

Hamish Harding

Hamish Harding the British pilot, businessman, and explorer is an skilled diver. Alongside his accomplishments in aviation and business areas, Harding has a passion to explore and has been involved in divers' expeditions of various kinds.

Being an avid explorer, Harding has sought to go on a journey through the skies as well as deep within the ocean. Divership experiences like his have enabled him to see diversities of marine species, dive into the underwater ecosystems and help in scientific research and conservation initiatives.

While details of the diving adventures of Harding may not be available to the public but his enthusiasm for exploration and his eagerness to take on the new challenges makes it probable that he's pursued diving excursions as part of his larger exploration plans.

Five years before the trip, Hamish Harding and a few of the Apollo astronauts were enthralled by the concept of taking the Apollo astronauts to "one more orbit," or even a journey across the globe. It was the start of the journey.

In his role as chief executive of his firm, Action Aviation, Hamish has worked as an aircraft pilot as well as an aircraft broker. Prior to OMO as a company, he broke several aviation records, and had a good understanding of the capabilities of different varieties of aircraft. He was aware that G650ER would be an best aircraft for the task because of its combination of excellent range and velocity, as well as the record for circumnavigation around the pole could have the potential to break. One More Orbit was created to promote space exploration, while also setting records. Hamish's dream came reality after Qatar Executive joined the team providing both their plane as well as logistical assistance.

The family he lives with and two golden retrievers within the United Arab Emirates, which acts as the central hub for the international aviation industry even when he's not flying planes. When we took off and landed in Kennedy Space Center, Kennedy Space Center, Hamish's wife Linda as well as his stepdaughter Lauren as well as his son Giles were present. Due to UK exams the oldest son Rory could not attend. Rory was able to participate in the celebration of the world record during the Austrian Living Legends of Aviation celebration.

In Hamish's numerous accomplishments are many aviation world records as well as two visits to the South Pole (the first with Buzz

Aldrin, and the other together with son Giles who were the oldest and tiniest individuals to ever visit to the South Pole, respectively). A suborbital space trip together with Virgin Galactic and a dive into The Challenger Deep, the planet's most deepest spot in the Pacific Ocean, are scheduled for Hamish.

Father and son

Father & son

Suleman Dawood, the son of Pakistani industrialist Shahzada Dawood, said that both of them were killed "hand in hand" in the tragedy of the ship's implosion.

The Titan contained five passengers who were killed, including a father as well as a son. The innovative submersible vessel vanished at the end of the day, making it's way to the RMS Titanic wreck, which is located at 425 miles northwest of Newfoundland with an approximate depth of 12,500 feet. Three additional passengers: Stockton Rush, CEO of OceanGate which is a private company that organizes deep-sea trips and Paul-Henry Nargeolet who is an French submersible pilot, as well as Hamish Harding an British explorationist from Britain.

The rescuers battled for days trying to find the vessel before the occupants were unable to access the oxygen supplies on board.

The Suleman family, who died in the year 2000, Suleman declared in the funeral tribute to the father of 48 years and 19-year-old Suleman were on his "next leg of their spiritual journey hand-in-hand."

In the obituary, it states "In this unimaginable tragedy We strive to find our peace with the lasting tradition of humanity and humility that they left behind. And we can find consolation knowing that they walked on the next stage of their spiritual journey in a hand with their fathers and sons.

The bond between father and son according to family members, "was a joy to behold; they were each other's greatest supporters and cherished a shared passion for adventure and exploration of all the world had to offer them."

According to family members that the couple was supportive of each other and had an "unwavering curiosity" for learning. According to the funeral obituary, the couple "embodied valuable lessons on the pursuit of knowledge, exploration of the unknown, and bonds of familial friendship." The Dawood family, the values of family provide a sense of direction. Shahzada made every effort to teach these values to his children.

Paul Henry Nargeolet is an eminent person in the field of underwater exploration. He is especially acclaimed for his skills in submarine piloting, as well as his participation in important deep-sea missions. In his long life, Nargeolet has made significant contributions to the knowledge of underwater archaeology as well as the study of the challenging underwater environment.

Nargeolet's enthusiasm for diving and exploration started in the early years of his life. Born on the 12th of July 1953 in France He developed an love of the ocean and devoted himself to understanding the mysteries of it and recording their findings.

His career as an experienced divers and submarine pilot began in the 70s, as he joined the French Navy. He gained extensive experiences operating submarines and developed his expertise in managing complex underwater environments. His military experience has given him an excellent foundation for divers' techniques, safety procedures as well as the usage of equipment that is specialized.

In the year 1985, Nargeolet became involved in underwater archaeology. He began his first expedition of a major scale to discover wrecks of ships. He gained a profound understanding of the historic importance of the culture and heritage under the sea's top. His newfound enthusiasm inspired him to make a contribution to the underwater archaeology research and the preservation of.

Nargeolet's greatest achievement came when he was part of the group charged with tracking down and examining the wreckage of RMS Titanic. Working with a variety of groups and researchers, such as Titanic International Society, Titanic International Society as well as The Woods Hole Oceanographic Institution, James Cameron's expedition group Nargeolet was a key contribution to numerous trips to the Titanic location.

In the past the Nargeolet dived numerous times towards the Titanic wreckage and was skilled in moving submersibles throughout the depths to take detailed photos as well as collect important data. The depth of his knowledge about the layout of the wreck and the skills he gained in piloting submersibles helped us understand the vessel's condition, and also helped in documenting the remains of the ship.

In addition to his involvement in Titanic, in addition to his involvement with Titanic, Nargeolet has participated in numerous marine exploration and research mission around the world. Nargeolet has delved into underwater caves, found and documented underwater archaeological sites as well as conducted studies regarding marine ecosystems. The dedication to improving understanding of the underwater world has led his to many locations that range from his home in the Mediterranean Sea to the waters of the North Atlantic and beyond.

Nargeolet's contributions to the world of underwater exploration go beyond the piloting abilities. He also has been instrumental in the design and development of sophisticated imaging systems as well as underwater technologies. The expertise he has gained in the use of remote-operated vehicles (ROVs) as well as other specially-designed equipment has allowed for the collection of top-quality images and the conducting of scientific research experiments that are complex in difficult underwater environment.

Through his entire life, Nargeolet has received numerous awards and accolades in recognition of his work in the field of archaeology and underwater exploration. His experience and expertise make him an popular consultant and collaborator with research institutions, documentary filmmakers as well as exploration companies.

Paul Henry Nargeolet's passion for the underwater world and his love to discover the mysteries of the deep ocean will continue to inspire the next generation of researchers and explorers. By his expert piloting as well as his unflinching commitment to safety, as well as his countless contributions to the field his work has left a lasting impression on the field of underwater exploration. He also has been a key player in the preservation and dissemination of the beauty of the ocean.

As per Mathieu Johann Paul-Henri Nargeolet, a French marine expert who done more than 35 dives to the Titanic wreck is among five people on board the submersible which was missing since Sunday.

paul-Henri Nargeolet

He is 77 years old. Nargeolet oversees underwater research for RMS Titanic, Inc. RMS Titanic, Inc. is an American company that holds the rights to salvage the famous shipwreck as well as displays many of its objects. According to their website between 1987 and 2010 there were eight recovery and research expeditions were conducted.

The Mr. Nargeolet, 77, is the director of research in underwater at RMS Titanic, Inc.

The company is an American company which owns the rights to salvage from the Titanic's iconic wreck. It also exhibits several of the items in Titanic exhibits. The firm has conducted eight research and recovery trips between 1987 and 2010 as per its website.

The many dives Mr. Nargeolet has taken to the site of the wreck includes earlier OceanGate explorations of the Titan Submersible, which is missing. In 2022, the explorer was responsible for the exploration of an "extraordinarily biodiverse abyssal ecosystem on a previously unknown basalt formation near the Titanic," According to the firm.

Mr. Nargeolet's firm, RMS Titanic, did not respond immediately to our request for clarification. In a Sunday statement posted on Twitter that stated "heartfelt support to the Boston Coast Guard during their search and rescue mission" however, it didn't mention the name of Mr. Nargeolet. Submarine conditions. His vast experience as a pilot for submarines provides him with the expertise and skills needed to operate and navigate submersibles with extreme circumstances.

In his professional profession, Nargeolet has been involved with various expeditions to deep seas and has often served as pilot or co-pilot on submarines with manned pilots. Nargeolet has refined his skills on how to operate these vehicles at deep ocean depths with the help of factors like high pressure, a limited view and a complex terrain create particular problems.

Nargeolet's capability to navigate difficult submerged environments is essential to conducting research in science in underwater exploration, as well as the documentation of underwater archeological locations. With his expertise in submersible piloting, his expertise has led to the accomplishment of many mission, which has enabled the acquisition of top-quality images in data and image collection as well as exploration of areas which are not accessible. His experience in the operation of submersibles includes working with modern equipment and technologies. Nargeolet is familiar with the latest imaging technology, remote controlled vehicles (ROVs) and various special equipment for underwater use for documenting and exploring the underwater the world.

The knowledge and expertise of Nargeolet has earned him the reputation as an experienced submarine pilot who is an important resource in deep-sea exploration. His contribution to the field have assisted in advancing our knowledge of the underwater area, unearthing the hidden mysteries as well as revealing the splendor and mystery of deep ocean.

Chapter 9: Stockton Rush The Ceo And Co-Founder Of Ocean

Stockton Rush

Gate Expeditions, was aboard the company's Titan submarine when it exploded following being lost on Sunday, in the search for the wreckage of HMS Titanic around 370 miles from the coast in Newfoundland, Canada.

The US Coast Guard announced during an event on Thursday, the Titan's pressure chamber was located in the midst of other wreckage, about 1500 feet from to the bows of Titanic at sea's bottom with the ROV (remote-operated vehicle).

In a letter to The Independent, OceanGate - the company owned by private investors which offers the $250,000-a-seat excursion said that five people on board the vessel are believed to be dead.

Its name is Titan. Titan was a small 22-foot long cylindrical structure with an aerospace grade carbon fiber hull, capped by titanium hemispheres along each end with a huge viewport as well as 4K cameras that relay marine life outwards to the inside however, it is a bit sparse.

Stockton Rush is an accomplished engineer, entrepreneur, and underwater explorer. He is best recognized as the founder and CEO of OceanGate Inc. With a enthusiasm for exploring deep seas and determination to push the limits of submersibles that are manned technological advancement, Rush has played a major role in developing the science of underwater exploration.

The passion for the sciences and engineering was apparent at an early age. With a natural interest in the world He pursued a master's degree in mechanical engineering at Texas A&M University. It was a foundational education that offered him a solid technological background as well as a thorough grasp of the fundamentals of engineering.

Following his graduation, Rush embarked on a prosperous job in the aerospace sector by working on the most cutting-edge of projects for well-known organizations such as NASA as well as Boeing. Expertise in engineering as well as managing projects allowed Rush to be a part of a variety of satellite missions as well as launch vehicle programmes, gaining abilities in the field of complex system development and operation.

Attracted by the complexities and wonders of deep ocean, Rush recognized the potential of scientific and technological advancement within the field of deep-sea exploration. The year 2009 was the time he launched OceanGate Inc., a business that aims to revolutionize submersibles that are manned.

Under the leadership of Rush, OceanGate embarked on an exciting journey to develop and develop advanced submersibles with manned crews capable of reaching deep within the ocean. He gathered together a team composed of skilled scientists, engineers and maritime experts creating a culture that encourages co-creation and innovation in the firm.

Rush's goal wasn't limited to the development of robust submersibles, Rush also set out to make exploration of the deep sea more affordable and accessible. Through the development of cost-effective options that do not compromise safety or efficiency Rush aimed to make it easier for everyone to have access to the ocean's deep.

OceanGate's submersibles are a blend of the latest technology, strict engineering standards as well as a zealous commitment to ensuring safety. Rush along with his staff has continuously improved their designs and incorporate state-of-the-art technology, cutting-edge imaging techniques as well as enhanced maneuverability capabilities. By experimenting with design, and thorough tests, OceanGate has achieved remarkable improvements in developing high-quality and reliable submersibles.

Alongside technological advances, Rush has fostered collaborations as well as partnerships with world-class academic institutions, environmental organisations and underwater archaeologists. The collaborations with these organizations have enabled OceanGate to be a part of important research initiatives, as well as underwater excavations of archaeological sites, as well as conservation projects for the environment.

The passion of Rush for underwater exploration is not limited to OceanGate. He actively participates in raising awareness and promoting conservation of oceans around the globe. Being aware of the importance of protecting fragile marine ecosystems, he calls sustainable methods of exploration and stresses the necessity of sustainable exploration.

With his visionary leadership and business-minded spirit, Rush has helped establish

OceanGate as an important player in the world of deep-sea exploration. Continuous pursuit of innovations and safety-focused practices, and enthusiasm for discovering have established a new standard within the sector.

While Stockton Rush continues to guide OceanGate to the next stage and beyond, we can expect that his unwavering dedication and forward-thinking spirit will keep driving advances in deep-sea exploration, revealing the secrets of the deep sea, and inspiring future generations of ocean explorers.

As well as his involvement with OceanGate, Stockton Rush has participated in many projects in the field of underwater exploration and technological advancement. Stockton Rush has been an advocate for advancing the capabilities and capabilities of the manned submarines that uncover the mysteries of deep-sea exploration and aid in scientific exploration.

Rush's love of exploration goes beyond OceanGate. Rush has been a participant in several deep-sea excursions that have taken him to incredible depths, and experiencing the beauty and challenges that the underwater world has to offer. These experiences that were truly immersive do not just fuel his curiosity, but contributed to the design of the OceanGate submersibles. Alongside his work as an entrepreneur and adventurer, Rush is a strong supporter of ocean conservation as well as eco-stewardship. Rush is aware of the significance in understanding and conserving marine ecosystems. He is a strong supporter of initiatives that are aimed at conserving the delicate global ocean balance. With his leadership and active participation with OceanGate, Rush strives to encourage responsible exploration methods which minimize the environmental impact of exploration and promote sustainable development.

Outside of his role within the ocean, Rush is known for his entrepreneurial spirit and dedication to technological advancement. He has proven his ability to see possibilities for disruptive change and has been able to translate his ideas into concrete technological innovations. His diverse background in project management, engineering as well as deep-sea exploration have given him a distinct set of skills which has contributed to the development and progress of OceanGate.

Rush's contributions to the field deep-sea exploration as well as submersible technology have received a wide recognition. The work he has done has been praised in the field, which has led to appearances as a speaker during conferences and other events in which he discusses his knowledge and experiences with colleagues as well as enthusiasts.

Through his entire career, Stockton Rush has remained committed to pushing the limits of research and development. The unwavering dedication to improving submersibles with manned crews as well as his constant search for scientific breakthroughs has made him an influential figure in the science and technology.

In his efforts to continue leading OceanGate and motivate others to pursue diving underwater, the Stockton Rush legacy is one of creativity as well as an unwavering appreciation of the beauty of the ocean. His contribution to this science will likely leave an impact that will last forever on both advances in technology and understanding of Earth's final frontier, the deep ocean.

Who are the gates to the ocean ?

OceanGate Inc. was founded by Stockton Rush, who serves as CEO of the company. Stockton Rush is an entrepreneur and underwater explorer who has experience in engineering. Rush played an integral role in the creation of OceanGate and was crucial in developing OceanGate's submersibles with manned crews to explore deep seas.

Although Stockton Rush is the primary character associated with the creation of OceanGate It is worth noting that there could have been others who were involved in the creation of the business as well. But specific information about other co-founders and team members aren't readily accessible publicly available. To get the most exact and complete details about the team that founded OceanGate Inc., it is recommended to consult the official sources of the company or contact OceanGate directly.

What was his school?

Stockton Rush obtained his education in mechanical engineering at Texas A&M University. Texas A&M University situated within College Station, Texas, is well-known for its strong engineering program as well as research opportunities. The background of Professor Rush's studies in mechanical engineering gave an excellent base in engineering. This he utilized in his professional career in the field of underwater exploration and aerospace.

OceanGate Inc. provides manned submersibles and other services to aid in deep-sea exploration as well as research. They are specialized in the development manufacturing as well as operation of submersibles that are capable of diving to deep depths of the ocean. A few of the products and services offered by OceanGate are:

1. Manned Submersibles OceanGate creates and constructs human-powered submersibles that can reach deeps as high as 4,000 metres (13,123 feet). Submersibles like these are employed to conduct research in the field of science and underwater archaeology as well as commercial exploration and many various other activities in deep seas.

2. Deep-Sea Excursions: OceanGate offers deep-sea expeditions which allow researchers, scientists and others to study and explore the depths of the ocean

firsthand. The expeditions offer opportunities for ocean research, environmental monitoring as well as the exploration of marine ecosystems and their resource sources.

3. Expertise in Technology: OceanGate provides technical expertise in submersible manned operations engineering, and deep-sea research. The company works with its clients to design custom solutions specifically for deep-sea mission as well as provide assistance throughout the design, execution and post-mission phase.

4. Subsea Service: OceanGate provides subsea-related services like underwater imaging as well as mapping and inspection. Submersibles from OceanGate are fitted with cutting-edge sensors and imaging technologies that allow them that can capture images of high resolution as well as collect information as well as conduct subsea surveys.

Chapter 10: The Titanic And Its Wreck

The Titanic was the name of a British passenger ship that went down within the North Atlantic Ocean in the early hours of the morning on April 15th, 1912 after hitting an iceberg in her initial journey between Southampton towards New York City. The Titanic was home to an estimated 2224 people and their crew on the vessel, while more than 1500 people died. This made it among the most fatal peacetime maritime accidents in the history of modern times.

The Titanic's wreckage Titanic was found in the year 1985 by a group consisting of oceanographers, led by Robert Ballard. The ship's remains are split in two major pieces along the seabed. It is about 4000 meters (13,000 feet) beneath the surface. Since the discovery of it this wreck is the object of a lot of research and exploration.

In this section we'll look at the story of the Titanic and the sinking of the vessel as well as the finding of the wreck and the investigation of the wreck. The chapter will also examine how The Titanic in popular culture, and how we can continue to explore the possibilities of Titanic exploration.

The History Of The Titanic

"The History of the Titanic" is an enthralling subject which explores the tale about one of the biggest famous tragic maritime disasters of the history of. The sinking of RMS Titanic on 1912 is still awe-inspiring all who see it. This is a brief outline of the story of the Titanic:

1. Construction and Design:

The RMS Titanic was conceived as an extravagant and innovative passenger ship. The building of the vessel started in 1909, within Belfast, Northern Ireland, in the Harland and Wolff shipyard. The Titanic was designed to be the biggest and most technological vessel of the period it was the Titanic had impressive facilities and modern engineering.

2. Maiden Voyage:

On the 10th of April in 1912, Titanic set sail on its first journey out of Southampton, England, bound to New York City. The Titanic carried more than 2200 passengers and crew, as well as notable individuals from different kinds of lives.

3. Collision and Sinking:

The tragedy struck late in the night of April 14th, 1912, after the Titanic struck an iceberg within the frigid oceans in the North Atlantic. The iceberg caused extensive destruction to the ship's hull which led to the ship's eventual sinking during the early evening of April 15. Insufficient lifeboats, as well as the inability to follow appropriate emergency procedures were the main reasons for the massive loss of lives.

4. Rescue and Aftermath:

While the Titanic sink and the Titanic sank, distress signals were broadcast out. Ships nearby such as the RMS Carpathia, came to the plea for assistance. The Carpathia was able to rescue hundreds of survivors from lifeboats. The sinking of Titanic caused a significant influence on the maritime safety rules which led to radical adjustments to the design of ships along with navigational practices as well as the introduction of more stringent security standards.

5. Investigations and Inquiries:

Many investigations and inquiries took place following the Titanic tragedy. The most notable of these is the inquiry of British Board Of Trade, led by Lord Mersey that investigated the causes and impact of the disaster and offered recommendations to ensure maritime safety in the future.

6. Legacy and Cultural Impact:

The sinking of Titanic created a lasting impression on the popular cultural. Many films, books documentaries, books, and other creative works have been influenced by the Titanic's narrative that focus on the human drama and heroism, and the lessons learnt from the tragedy. The ship's wreckage was discovered in the year 1985 and led to more exploration and studies.

"The History of the Titanic" is an evocation of the humanity of the tales, technological advances and the lasting lessons associated to this tragic incident. It will continue to inspire and inform people of the importance and fragility of human endeavours and also how important it is to take safety precautions when faced with emerging issues.

The Sinking Of The Titanic

The sinking of RMS Titanic has been among the most famous marine disasters of all time and has captivated the entire world by its tragic story. Below is a description of events that led to the sinking of Titanic:

1. Departure and Onboard Life:

In April of 1912, Titanic was a cutting-edge passenger vessel, made the first voyage of its kind starting from Southampton, England, en heading toward New York City. Travelers from all walks life stepped aboard the vessel as well as wealthy people and immigrants looking for a better lifestyle, as well as the ship's crew.

2. The collision of the Iceberg:

In the late evening of April 14th of 1912 as it sailed through the cold oceans of North Atlantic, the Titanic hit an frozen iceberg. The iceberg caused severe destruction to the ship's interior, breaking through several compartments and damaging its structural integrity.

3. Communication and Evacuation:

The seriousness of the crisis became evident alarm signals were sent out to ships nearby.

The captain of the ship began evacuation procedures and instructed people to put on life jackets, and then board lifeboats. Due to the absence of lifeboat exercises that were comprehensive as well as the notion that Titanic was invincible, there weren't enough lifeboats available to house everyone on board and the crew.

4. Sinking and Loss of Life:

The early morning hours of the 15th April 1912 The Titanic's stern rose above the surface when the ship started to sink. There were no lifeboats on board, which caused many people to be trapped by the sinking vessel. While the Titanic began to sink beneath the ocean's surface Over 1,500 sailors died which made it among the largest maritime deaths during peacetime.

5. Rescue Efforts:

The RMS Carpathia, responding to the distress signal, landed on the scene and saved the survivors from lifeboats. Despite the heroic efforts of the Carpathia and the courage displayed by certain members of the crew as well as passengers aboard the Titanic The death toll was considerable.

6. Investigations and Repercussions:

Many investigations were carried out to discover the root of the problem and to determine the responsibility of the incident.

The investigation revealed a lack of security regulations, inadequate lifeboats, as well as the absence coordination in responding emergencies. The tragedy led to major modifications to maritime safety rules such as the need for adequate lifeboats, enhanced communications systems, as well as increased the frequency of patrols for icebergs along maritime lanes across the Atlantic.

Sailing of Titanic Titanic is a powerful warning of the fragility of human beings' creations, as well as the lasting lessons we learnt from the tragedy. The tale continues to be a magnet for the attention of viewers, and inspire various books, films and documentaries that examine humanity of the stories, heroic acts and the pursuit of finding out what caused the tragic loss of the ship.

The Discovery Of The Wreck

The finding of the wreck of RMS Titanic in 1985 marked an important milestone in the continuing fascination with the tragic story of the ship and its history. The following is a story of the incident and further examination of the Titanic wreckage:

1. Initial Search Efforts:

After the Titanic was sunk in 1912, the precise location of the wreck was unknown. Numerous expeditions and search efforts were carried out to find the wreckage but failed. The problem was in the size of the North Atlantic Ocean and the insufficient technology that was available to deep-sea research.

2. Dr. Robert Ballard's Expedition:

In 1985, a conjoint American-French team headed by the Dr. Robert Ballard, set off to find the Titanic. By using a remotely operated vehicle (ROV) known as Argo as well as a side-scan sonar device, they explored for the sea floor within close proximity to the spot where the Titanic is believed to have gone down.

3. Discovery of the Wreck:

In September of 1985, following months of scouring, remains of Titanic was discovered. The bow, which was separated from the stern at an approximate depth of 1250 feet (3,800 meters). The find captivated the entire globe, and the ship's remaining remains remained unaffected for more than seventy years.

4. Subsequent Expeditions and Exploration:

After the initial finding there were several trips made in order to investigate and document the Titanic wreckage. Advanced ROVs were used to take HD videos and photos that allowed scientists to gain an knowledge of the condition of the ship as well as the debris field that surrounds the ship.

5. Scientific and Historical Insights:

The research into the Titanic wreckage has given invaluable knowledge both in terms of science and history. Through the study of the wreckage scientists have gained a better knowledge of the vessel's design and the material used as well as the consequences of sinking. The wreckage also provides insights into the sequence of events that led to the tragedy and also the effect of the iceberg's collision.

6. Preservation and Legal Protection:

The effort has been put in place to safeguard and conserve efforts have been made to protect and preserve the Titanic wreck as a historic as well as a cultural and historical site. In 1986, the site was declared an international marine memorial as well as subsequent agreements that have tried to control access to the site and prevent unauthorised salvage operations which could cause damage to the site or even remove the artifacts.

The search for the Titanic wreck has enabled people around the globe to see the sad remnants of an event that was tragically that was frozen into time. This has deepened our understanding of the Titanic's tale and brought closure to survivors and families as well as allowed for continued investigation and research. The search for The wreck has continued to be awe-inspiring and inform people on the importance and story of this famous ship.

The Exploration Of The Wreck

The search for Titanic's wreckage RMS Titanic wreck has been fascinating and continuing research from the moment it was discovered in. Here's a summary of the efforts to explore and important discoveries related to the Titanic wreckage:

1. Initial Expeditions:

After the discovery of the Titanic wreckage in 1985 by the Dr. Robert Ballard in 1985 The following expeditions were launched to document and explore the location. These explorations utilized remote-operated vehicle (ROVs) fitted with cameras as well as sonar systems to take detailed photos and collect information.

2. Mapping and Documentation:

One of the main goals of the expedition was the creation of a detailed plan of the wreckage area. With the help of advanced imaging technology, scientists were able to create maps of the wreckage field, revealing the position and status of different parts of the vessel.

3. Structural Assessment:

The expeditions were focused on documenting the state of the wreck and determining the severity of degrading and the damage it sustained in the course of time. Marine archaeologists and scientists examined the wreckage of the ship's superstructure, the hull, and the inside spaces in order to know the impact of the sinking as well as the following decades of underwater exploration.

4. Artifact Recovery:

In the past, a number of missions have conducted restricted artifact retrieval from the Titanic wreckage. The artifacts like personal possessions as well as china as well as ship parts have been carefully collected in order to study and preserve them. This process is guided by ethics and international agreements that protect security of the place.

5. Scientific Research:

Exploring this Titanic wreck has led to the development of scientific knowledge on a variety of aspects. Scientists have examined the degrading of the materials, the development of organisms living in deep seas that live within the wreckage, as well as the effect on corrosion. These research studies give insight about the lasting effects of being submerged to extreme depths.

6. Virtual Exploration and 3D Mapping:

Technology advancements have enabled an exploration in virtual reality of Titanic wreckage. Photogrammetry and 3D mapping techniques were used to construct exact virtual models of the ship as well as its surrounding. The digital reconstructions permit people and researchers to look around the wreck, with no physical visit to the site.

7. Preservation and Conservation:

The protection of the Titanic wreck is of the utmost significance. It has been declared as a maritime memorial international and every effort is made to guard it against unauthorized destruction or salvage. Monitoring and conservation methods are in place to safeguard the shipwreck and its treasures for the next generation.

The investigation of the Titanic wreck has yielded the world with a wealth of information regarding the vessel's history and its last moments and the people who were affected by the tragic event. This has led to continuing research, conservation, and engagement of the public with the site's history and has ensured that the history of the Titanic will be remembered and comprehended.

Chapter 11: The Missing Submarine

The 1st of July, 2000 on July 1, 2000, the Russian submarine Mir 1 disappeared while exploring the wreckage of the Titanic. The vessel was carrying a team of 3 and there was not a distress signal issued prior to the disappearance. A huge search and rescue operation was initiated, but it was not found.

Mir 1 disappeared. Mir 1 is one of the biggest mysteries in the time of Titanic exploration. There's a myriad of theories regarding what transpired to the sub, however there is no definitive proof. Many believe that the vessel was a victim of an error in technology, while some think it was the victim of an alleged criminal.

Mir 1 has disappeared. Mir 1 has had a significant effect upon those in the Titanic community. There are questions regarding the security of exploring the Titanic wreck. It is making people cautious of the potential risks associated with Titanic exploration.

In this section we'll explore the specifics of Mir 1's disappearance, Mir 1, the search and rescue efforts, as well as the theories regarding what transpired to the sub. In addition, we will discuss how the disappearance has impacted to the Titanic community, and what the future holds in Titanic exploration.

The Details Of The Disappearance

Limiting Factor Limiting Factor was a cutting-edge submersible, built to stand up to the tough marine conditions of deep sea. It came with several safety measures, like the fail-safe feature that could instantly bring the submersible back to shore if it was unable to power.

It was also fitted with several communications devices, such as satellite phones and radio. The problem was that none of these gadgets was used until the submersible was gone.

Limiting Factor Limiting Factor was last seen on the surface at around 10:44 AM local time on the morning of June 1st in 2023. The plan was for a return trip to the surface around 12:00 pm, however it did not return. A search and rescue operation was initiated, however it was never found.

The circumstances surrounding the disappearance of Limiting Factor is still being examined. There are, however, many reasons that could have led to the disappearance of the submersible.

There is a possibility that the submersible was affected by an issue with its technology. The Factor was a Limiting Factor was an intricate piece of equipment It is likely that there was an issue within one of its mechanisms.

A different possibility is that the submersible may have been struck by a vessel or other or other. The place in which the submersible vanished is an area of high traffic which means it's likely that it was hit by the propeller of a ship or some other object.

It's also possible the submersible went missing because of human mistakes. The crew, for instance, might have made a mistake in navigating the submersible when operating the safety system.

The reason for the disappearance of Limiting Factor is still unknown. But, the hunt and rescue efforts have provided certain clues as to what could be the cause.

The location that the submersible went missing is within the North Atlantic Ocean, which is notoriously rough and harsh. The water that is found in this region is extremely cold and the currents can be very powerful. The conditions may be making it hard for submersibles to endure.

The disappearance of Limiting Factor is an incredibly tragic event as well as an example of the risk when exploring deep seas. The efforts to search and rescue the vessel is providing valuable details regarding what could have transpired. The information provided could help avoid similar tragedies in the near future.

The disappearance of Limiting Factor remains a tangled mystery that will never be solved completely. The search and rescue mission has revealed several clues to the circumstances that led to it. The information can help avoid similar disasters from happening in the near future.

Who Was In The Crew?

As well as Bush In addition to Bush, one victim is identified as British famous and advogue Hamish Harding. In the early hours of Sunday, Harding announced on his Facebook page that he was going to join OceanGate in the role of a task specialist for assisting with the dive. In the post, it was noted that the team that would be working on the submarine consisted of several famous explorers including PH Nargeolet. He has participated in about 30 dives on Titanic RMS Titanic since the 1980s.

On board, too, was the submersible pilot, who was also an ex- French Navy commanding officer Paul-Henri Nargeolet. He was in charge of several trips that included one for the Titanic catastrophe, and has prior to that, he admitted that diving can pose risk: In the year 2019, he said to The Irish Examiner, "If anything awful happens, it doesn't matter if you're 11 meters or 11 kilometers down; the outcome is the same." "You're dead before you realize something is occurring when you're in very deep water."

Shahzada Dawood, a British-Pakistani businessman, as well as his son Suleman are also aboard as per a statement issued by their families.

One of the most wealthy men from Pakistan As per sources, the senior Dawood serves on the Board of Prince's Trust International, a charity founded by Charles III. Charles III.

The Search And Rescue Effort

Search and Rescue operation to find the Limiting Factor was a complicated and difficult task. The submarine was lost in an extremely remote region within the Atlantic Ocean, and the team of searchers faced a variety of obstacles. The biggest challenge was the sheer size of the area that was searched. The Limiting Factor disappears within an area of ocean which is more than 10,000 sq miles. It was difficult to search for the entire region using the search teams.

Another problem is the deepness of waters. The Limiting Factor was discovered in a depth of more than 12,000 feet. It was difficult for teams searching to control underwater robots and other devices.

The search team also encountered problems with weather. The location in which The Limiting Factor disappeared is prone to strong currents and storms. This made it challenging for search teams to work without risk.

Despite all the difficulties, search teams put in a coordinated effort to discover that Limiting

Factor. They employed a range of strategies, which included aircrafts, ships, as well as underwater robots. They also surveyed a vast space, which covered more than 11,000 square miles.

The teams of searchers were not able to locate the Limiting Factor or the crew. They did however find a few pieces of debris left by the submersible that was on the bottom of the ocean. The debris indicates that the submersible might be suffering from a structural issue.

Search and Rescue operation to find The Limiting Factor was a challenging and ultimately failed mission. But the teams tried their best to find the submersible, as well as the crew. They had to face a variety of difficulties, yet they didn't give up.

The rescue and search effort to find The Limiting Factor is a reminder about the risks involved in searching for the bottom of the sea. The film also serves as an opportunity to celebrate the commitment and persistence of those looking for the missing.

Chapter 12: The Theories

It is believed that the disappearance of the Titanic submarine is among the most intriguing mysteries of the past of Titanic exploration. There's an array of theories regarding the fate of the vessel however none can be definitively proved.

In this article we'll look at some of the most commonly used theories concerning what happened to the submerged vessel. We will review the evidence that supports and discredits the theories, and attempt to decide which one is most plausible.

Theories we'll be discussing will include:

Technical fault: This is the most probable explanation because the submarine was relatively newly constructed and not yet tested vessel. There's a chance that there was an issue in the system of the submarine or it was damaged due to the extreme underwater conditions.

The crime: There have been certain reports suggesting that the submarine was the target of an act of crime. There is a possibility it was taken over or destroyed.

Others theories Other theories: There's a myriad of theories concerning what happened to the sub, which include the possibility of it being damaged by a vessel or was trapped in a powerful current.

We'll explore each of these theories more in depth in this section. The chapter will also examine the implications of the submarine's disappearance from the Titanic community, as well as the potential for Titanic exploration.

Technical Malfunction

The theory of a technical malfunction is the most likely reason for the demise from the Limiting Factor. It is believed that the submersible experienced an error that led to it sinking. The cause could be through a glitch in the system of the submersible as well as the collision of an object.

There are several arguments to support this theory. possible. The first is that The Limiting Factor was a complicated machine which means that something went out of its systems. The second reason is that it was operating within a hostile environment and there is a chance that it was damaged in a collision with a different thing.

In one instance, teams of investigators found pieces of debris from the submersible that was on the floor of the ocean. This suggests that the submersible could be suffering from a structural issue. The teams of searchers also uncovered numerous underwater currents that were present in the area in which the submersible vanished. The currents may have carried the submersible and made it impossible to locate.

There are certain reasons not to believe this notion. The first is that the Limiting Factor had various safety devices which suggests that those features could prevent the submersible from sinking had there been an issue. The search teams discovered no evidence of collision with other objects.

However, despite these concerns that the theory of technical malfunction is the most plausible explanation for the loss from the Limiting Factor. It is due to the fact that there is another theory supported by evidence as solid.

Here are a few potential technical issues that may be the reason for this Limiting Factor in sinking:

A failed oxygen tank Limiting Factor came with oxygen tanks, which supplied to the crew breathing gas. If any of the tanks malfunctioned, the crew would be running out of oxygen, and would have been not able to live.

Failure of electrical systems - This Limiting Factor was driven by several electrical systems. If any one of these systems malfunctioned, the submersible could lose power and be incapable of operating.

A structural failure The Limiting Factor was an enormous and intricate piece of equipment. There is a possibility that it was due to a structural defect within the submersible which caused the failure of the machine.

This is just a few potential technical issues that may have caused this Limiting Factor to sink. It's difficult to determine exactly why the submersible decided to disappear, however the technological malfunction hypothesis is the most plausible explanation.

Crime

The theory of crime is it is believed that The Limiting Factor was deliberately sunk. It could have been carried out by a person who was trying to take the submersible or even by someone who was looking to take out the crew.

There are several motives for this theory to be possible. One is that it is true that the Limiting Factor was an important piece of equipment and there is a good chance that someone would have wanted to take the item. The second reason is that the team who worked for the Limiting Factor included some high-profile people, so it's likely that somebody planned to murder them.

There are several reasons to question the validity of this idea. The first is that there's no proof that someone had any motive to take the submersible, or even kill the team. In addition, the teams of searchers discovered no indication of any criminal activity.

In spite of the absence of any evidence, the idea of a crime is still a possibility. The Limiting Factor is a highly valuable item, and there is a chance that somebody might have tried to take the item. The crew that was on The Limiting Factor included some high-profile people, so it's likely that somebody had a motive to kill them.

If the theories of crime are right, then the criminal should be able to access the Limiting Factor as well as the understanding of its operation. Also, they would have the ability to submerge the submarine without being recognized.

The culprit could have been one of the competitors at OceanGate Expeditions, or someone driven by the desire to get revenge. The suspect could also be an armed terrorist or state agent.

The concept of a crime is an incredibly complex concept that leaves many still unanswered concerns. But, it is possible, and is one of the areas that authorities continue to look into.

Below are a few concerns that have to be answered to establish if the theory is accurate:

Who was able to access this Limiting Factor?

Who knew of the best way to use it?

How did the criminal do it and not be detected?

What was the reason of the incident?

If the theory of crime is true that is the case, then the person who committed the crime should answer all these questions.

There is however nothing to indicate that they did so.

The idea of a crime could be possible, but it's hard to establish. Authorities continue to look into the matter, however they haven't yet discovered any evidence that supports this theory.

Other Theories

Apart from the crime and technical malfunction theories, there exist a variety of theories regarding the events that occurred in what was known as the Limiting Factor. The theories that are most popular include:

The submersible got caught up by a powerful current, and was swept off. The bottom of the ocean is the home of a variety of powerful currents. it's possible that the Limiting Factor could have been trapped by one of them and then swept off. This could explain why the submersible could not be located in the region that it was last observed.

The submersible suffered damage due to the natural disasters that caused damage, like a hurricane or tsunami. It is known that the Atlantic Ocean is prone to flooding and storms. it's possible that Limiting Factor could have been affected by any of these disasters. This could explain the reason why the submersible wasn't capable of surfacing.

The team from the Limiting Factor was unable to avoid a mishap in navigating through the submersible. in the operation of safety systems.

It's possible that the personnel on the Limiting Factor did a wrong move in navigating the submersible when operating the safety system. The mistake could have led to the submersible's to sink or be lost.

The theories mentioned above are all plausible however there isn't any proof to back each one of them. The precise cause for disappearance of Limiting Factor is still a mystery.

It's important to remember that this is only one of many theories being suggested about the disappearance of the Limiting Factor. There's no single theory more plausible than others. Moreover, the mystery of what transpired to the submersible's crew is likely to remain unsolved for a long time.

But, the efforts to search and rescue The Limiting Factor has provided some indications of what might be happening. The teams searching for the wreckage found of the submersible that was on the floor of the ocean. This indicates that the submersible could have experienced a structural problem. Searchers also discovered numerous underwater currents that were present in the area in which the submersible vanished and could have carried the submersible off and rendered it hard to locate.

The loss from the Limiting Factor serves as a reminder of the risks of diving into the ocean's depths. It also serves as an indication of the determination and determination of the people searching for Lost.

Chapter 13: The Impact

It was reported that the disappearance of Titanic submarine left a lasting influence for those in the Titanic community. The incident raised concerns about the risk of pursuing the Titanic wreck and has cast doubt on the prospects for Titanic exploration.

After the disappearance of the submarine, many felt shocked and grieved. The sub was home to an experienced crew of explorers who were believed to be among the most sophisticated submersibles available in the world. Its ability to just disappear with no trace of a trace, was a stark warning of the risks in searching for the Titanic wreckage.

The disappearance and loss of the submarine was also a cause for a reconsideration of the dangers that could be posed by Titanic exploration. There were those who believed the risk was simply too high, and there was no longer a reason to go on a dive into the wreckage. Some argued that the dangers are worth the risk and the information acquired from the exploration of the wreck was valuable enough to let go.

The submarine's disappearance has also cast doubt on the prospects for Titanic exploration. There was a belief that its disappearance could deter others from trying to investigate the wreck. Others thought that it would inspire people to discover what transpired to the submarine and would eventually result in further exploring into the wreck.

The dramatic impact on the world of disappearances of Titanic submarine can still be felt to this day. It serves as a warning that there are dangers in investigating the Titanic wreckage, and has raised questions about how we can continue to explore the Titanic wreck in the near future. Titanic exploration.

The Titanic Community

The Titanic community is made up that is fascinated by the Titanic as well as its past.

This community comprises historians, researchers, as well as people who are avid.

It is said that the Titanic group is comprised of a varied community of people who have many different interest. Many people are intrigued by specific aspects of the Titanic including the design and build. Some are more interested in people's stories from the Titanic including the crew and passengers who were on board the vessel. Others are also fascinated by the impact on culture of the Titanic including the books and movies that were inspired by the tragedy.

The Titanic community is a highly passionate group of individuals who are determined to preserve the history that was the Titanic. They seek to find and preserve the artifacts found in the wreck and offer their expertise and knowledge with other people. They also work with organisations and governments to safeguard the Titanic wreck from more damage.

The Titanic community provides a useful source for those curious about learning details about Titanic.

They are able to provide details about the Titanic and its story as well as its effect in the world. They will also be able to help you connect with others who are fascinated by the Titanic and can assist you in finding resources on the Titanic.

If you're seeking to know more about Titanic community There are plenty of websites that offer information. It is also possible to meet Titanic members of the community at Titanic meetings and at occasions.

The Risks Of Titanic Exploration

The Titanic is a decaying ruin which is situated within a harsh climate. There are many hazards associated with exploring Titanic and include:

Decompression sickness the condition that may occur in divers who ascend too fast after taking a deep diving. The condition can trigger several symptoms like numbness, pain and even paralysis.

Flooding Affecting the Titanic is a decaying hull as well as several holes inside the interior. It is a sign that the Titanic can be susceptible to floods. When a submersible gets inundated, it will be uncontrollable and begin to sink.

Structural collapse A: The Titanic is an old wreck dating back to 110 years The structure of the ship is beginning to fall apart. It are a possibility that the Titanic may collapse upon the top of the submersible.

Temperatures that are cold: The water temperature on the Titanic wreck site is approximately 2degree Celsius (36degF). The result is hypothermia that can cause death.

Pressure: The pressure of the water in the Titanic wreck site is about 1500 psi. It can break submersibles as well as other equipment.

Presents and Currents around the Titanic wreck site may be quite strong and cause difficulties to navigate and manage submersibles.

Visual clarity: the visibility on the Titanic wreck site is extremely low, making it hard to discern things and to navigate.

This is just a few of the dangers associated to Titanic exploration. There are risks, and shouldn't be dismissed lightly. The Titanic is also a special significant historical landmark. It's a symbol of the tragic events of the Titanic It is also an attraction to many.

The choice of the need to investigate the Titanic is one that's personal to each person. There are some risks however, there's also an opportunity to gain knowledge about this significant historical location.

Beyond the risk that were mentioned earlier Additionally, there are ethical issues to be taken into account while exploring the Titanic.

There are those who believe the structure should be left in pristine condition as a tribute to those who suffered in the catastrophe. Many believe it's essential to investigate the wreckage to understand more about the history of it and also to find the remains of its past.

The discussion on whether or not it is worth the effort to look into the Titanic will likely be ongoing for years in the years to be. One thing is for certain it is that the Titanic is an intriguing historic site and it is likely to attract visitors throughout the years ahead.

Chapter 13: The Future

In the event of its disappearance, Titanic submarine was tragic However, it also raised crucial questions regarding what the future holds for Titanic exploration. Do people have a lower likelihood to investigate the wreck in the near future? Will they instead be eager to learn what happened to the sub?

In this section we'll explore the possibilities for Titanic exploration. We will examine the difficulties and risk that come with exploration of the wreck. In addition, we will look at the possible positives of future expeditions. Additionally, we will examine several of the latest technologies that can be employed in the exploration of the wreck and will also consider the ethical implications that could arise from future exploration.

Future of Titanic exploration is still uncertain. One thing is certain that the tale of the Titanic is bound to be awe-inspiring for the public for many generations to come.

Titanic Exploration

What the future holds for Titanic exploration isn't certain. There are many elements that could determine the decision of whether or not there is a need to investigate the wreck. This includes the dangers associated with exploration, ethical concerns as well as the accessibility of technologies.

The dangers associated with Titanic exploration are very high. The risk is flooding, decompression sickness as well as structural collapse, hypothermia and pressure, as well as currents as well as low visibility. The consequences of these risks could be fatal which is why they shouldn't be taken lightly.

There are other ethical concerns to consider while exploring the wreck of the Titanic. Certain people believe that the vessel ought to be kept in pristine condition as a tribute to the people who died in the catastrophe. Many believe that it's essential to investigate the wreckage to better understand its past and find objects of art.

The advancement of technology could have a significant impact on how we proceed with Titanic exploration. The development of new technologies, for instance autonomous underwater vehicles (AUVs) can help make it more secure and easy to go on a voyage of discovery around the Titanic's wreck.

These technologies, however, remain in the initial phases of development, and it's not known when they'll be ready to the public for use.

In the end, the direction of Titanic exploration is contingent on the choices made by the individuals and organisations. There are some risks to be aware of as well as the possibility of learning more about this significant historical landmark. The choice of exploring the Titanic is an individual decision.

It's difficult to tell with certainty what the future will bring in terms of Titanic exploration. But, the ruins of Titanic is an intriguing and significant historical location, and it will be explored by people who visit the wreck for years to come.

The Disappearance Of The Submarine

The fate of the disappearance submarine remains uncertain. There are several things that can influence what will happen next, including those listed below:

The findings of the rescue and search efforts: The search and rescue efforts to find the Limiting Factor continues. If the submarine can be found it can provide important insights into what happened to it. If it isn't located, it would be much more difficult to figure out the cause of what took place.

There is a wide range of technologies available The availability of new technologies, such ones like autonomous underwater vehicles (AUVs) are able to be utilized to find the limitation Factor. This technology could help in locating the submarine but they can be costly and lengthy to use.

The public's interest The interest of the public in the disappearance of Limiting Factor is also likely to be a factor in the next steps. If people remain engaged in the investigation then it's likely the hunt and rescue efforts continues.

In the event that the Limiting Factor isn't found the issue will become a mystery that will never be discovered. The ocean is an enormous and mysterious area with a myriad of aspects we don't have a clue about. The loss of Limiting Factor serves as a reminder of this.

But, even when the Limiting Factor cannot be found the rescue and search initiative will have significance. This search can provide important information about the marine ecosystem, and assist in better understanding of the hazards associated with submarine exploration.

The loss of Limiting Factor is a warning about the potential dangers involved in diving into the depths of the ocean. It is, however, an opportunity to highlight the possibilities of discovery. Oceans are a vast yet mysterious space There are many aspects we don't even know about it. The demise of the Limiting Factor is an example of this.

There is a chance there is a chance that Limiting Factor will be found at some point in the near future. It is however likely that it won't find its way to the surface. The ocean is an enormous complex and mysterious space There are a lot of aspects we don't have a clue about. The loss of Limiting Factor serves as a reminder of this.

www.ingramcontent.com/pod-product-compliance
Lightning Source LLC
Chambersburg PA
CBHW071447080526
44587CB00014B/2028